# Success Can Kill You

**One man's story of success, failure, faith and forgiveness**

By Rodney Jetton

PUBLISHED BY
THE RECOVERING POLITICIAN
http://TheRecoveringPolitician.com

## Also by Rodney Jetton

The Recovering Politician's Twelve Step Program to Survive Crisis (edited by Jonathan Miller)

Son of a Preacher Man: Growing up in the Seventies and Eighties

## DEDICATION

To my parents, Bill and Judy Jetton. Without your love, prayers and instruction growing up, I would not have made it through this life, and my eternal life would have ended in Hell.

Also to Paul Norman, a very smart kid who dedicated the best years of his life to helping me before leukemia took him from us at the age of 22. He was much wiser and better than I.

# Table of Contents

# Foreword

One Wednesday night I was ministering in my home church, The Sanctuary of Hope, and after teaching on the power of God and divine healing, I began to pray for people who needed healing. I was praying for people with back problems when a man I didn't know came up for prayer. After praying for his back, I asked him if it felt better. He said, "I'm a runner, and I'm going to check this out and see if it is real." A week later, I got a thank you note signed by Rodney Jetton saying the Lord had healed him when I prayed. I had no idea who Rodney Jetton was, so I asked my pastor if he knew him, and he told me Rodney was the former Speaker of the Missouri House of Representatives. This began a friendship with Rodney that continues to this day.

This book that he has written is the account of the great success that he had as Speaker of the House, and of how that same success almost destroyed him. This is the age-old story of success, failure, repentance and restoration. I have spent many hours with Rodney helping him better understand the Word of God as he walked the road of repentance and restoration. I have seen his devotion to the Word of God and his faithfulness in attending church, as well as his hunger for the Word of God. We have spent many hours together in my home, as I shared the things the Holy Spirit has taught me. My prayer is that Rodney's book will touch many lives as he shares his testimony.

Dr. Charles Shockley

# Introduction

The true measure of a person of God is not how purely they live their lives, but the way in which they react and respond to the revelations of the depths of their human nature – more aptly put, our personal and private sins.

When I first met Rod Jetton, I found a dear friend. Over time this friendship has had a huge and lasting impact on me. During my three decades of work with the people of the Missouri State Capitol, I have found that very few serve in public office and leave that position the same person that they were when first elected. Rod was no different than most, except that he has found his way back.

Like the vast majority of folks who work in the political arena, Rod started out with all the right motives and intentions. But faced with some of the most extreme situations (read his story for yourself), the end of the story is obvious: He is an even more humble man than he started out as. It is the details between the chapters, from beginning to end, that will make your mind swirl and maybe even cause you to ask questions of yourself.

I was aware of some very difficult struggles Rod had as he reached and excelled at the pinnacle of his political career. I was not only aware of some of his most intimate struggles that very few knew about at the time, but many of which Rod did not know I knew. Along with some of Rod's closest friends and family, I prayed for him and tried to watch his back from my limited position.

It pained me to watch a man I had come to love and care for get so lost in the wilderness of success. It pains me again to read the details that explain how it occurred. But most of all, it shames me that I failed to try harder to get through to my friend when I suspected that he was in trouble.

I was too comfortable and pacified by the thought that my dear friend needed to be left alone. After all, his time was very limited and he was playing a huge role in helping so many of us. I made it my business to watch from a distance and "not burden him" with too much prying. I made excuses for him when he was showing signs of distress. I defended him as others turned against him. Much like a naïve family member I empowered him by not demanding better accountability. By failing to take a tough love approach, I owe him my own apologies and ask for his forgiveness.

Now, a self-centered individual will blame others for their problems. Even though Rod dropped straight to the proverbial bottom of the barrel, he didn't drag everyone he could down with him. He focused on facing his own failures, and was able to see how to get back out. There are many stories through the centuries of others who, in principle, relate to Rod's experience. When you read the accounts of those who survived to tell their tale, they usually have the same focus as their turning point. Rod is no different in this regard. He tells it like it was, and is, without hiding any of his own shame.

Rod's transparency is a welcomed breath of fresh air. His self-portrait may not always be pretty, but it is an honest display of brokenness and humility. You will discover what I mean as you allow Rod to walk you through the chronology of his greatest successes, and how his personal failures slammed him into the bottom of his barrel. In many ways, his success almost killed him. Today he bears the scars of his gut-wrenching failures. As a contrast to the victory he now enjoys, he exposes these scars and the embarrassments beneath them.

Why does he do this? Rod does it because he did not climb out of that barrel alone! He wants to warn you about the simple excuses that led him down the wrong paths. And because he has a deep desire to share with you the victory that only comes from true repentance, and what that means in the real world.

The sad reality is that there are too many within the capitol culture and a great many more pursuing other dreams who can relate to Rod's story. The encouraging thought is that many of us may read the details of Rod's experience, and seeing ourselves in his mirror, might just refocus our own priorities. The dreadful fear is that many more will read his account and only see Rod.

Some will read Rod's account and question its accuracy, or criticize obscure details. Many will read because of a connectedness to the capitol culture. Some will reflect upon those personal connections. Over time most will read from a more detached or distant perspective. But all will face the primary question – will we heed Rod's story as a personal warning and embrace his advice?

The challenge I would put before every reader, curiosity seekers and truth learners alike, is that you read with an eye on your own mirror.

*"See then that ye walk circumspectly, not as fools, but as wise, redeeming the time, because the days are evil."*
*– Ephesians 5:15-16*

Kerry K. Messer
Founder, Missouri Family Network
Thirty-year veteran lobbyist
inside the capitol culture

# Preface

*"Let us weigh the gain and loss in wagering that God is, but let us consider the two possibilities. If you gain, you gain all; if you lose you lose nothing. Hesitate not then, to wager that He is." – Blaise Pascal*

In the movie Forrest Gump, the character Lt. Dan lost his legs in the Vietnam War and is bitter about it. He doesn't believe in God and makes a few comments ridiculing those who do. After another unsuccessful shrimping expedition and moments before a massive hurricane hits, Lt. Dan looks at Forrest and says, "Where the hell is this God of yours Gump?" To which a narrating Forrest Gump says, "It's funny Lieutenant Dan said that, 'cause right then, God showed up."

Sometimes in life, I have felt a lot like Lt. Dan. Now, I have always believed in God and my whole life I went to church, but there were times I wondered where God was. Did He really care about my problems? Was He actually paying attention to my life? I thought that maybe He was too busy working on more important things than to bother with my concerns. I should have remembered what Jesus said in Matthew 10:29-31, "Are not two sparrows sold for a farthing? And one of them shall not fall on the ground without your Father.

But the very hairs of your head are all numbered. Fear ye not therefore, ye are of more value than many sparrows."

Whatever doubts I had about God and His interest in my life were wiped away when He was there for me when I cried out for help in my troubles. Just like Lt. Dan, I was bitter about life but then "God showed up." When life was good and success was easy I believed in God and knew He was up there somewhere watching over me, but I didn't need much help from Him then. When my troubles hit and I had nowhere else to turn I experienced God's help first hand, which has given me a much stronger faith in God and His love for all people!

On December 7, 2009, I was arrested for felony assault after a one-night stand with a woman I met on Facebook. Soon after that, I received a call from a recent girlfriend telling me she was pregnant and I was going to be a daddy at age 42. Then just a few weeks later, I found out I was the target of a grand jury investigation from my handling of a bill when I was the Missouri Speaker of the House.

In less than one year I had gone from being one of the most powerful men in Missouri with a picture-perfect family to being divorced, without a job, facing serious criminal charges, and possible jail time. On top of all those problems, I was going to be responsible for a new baby.

By fall 2010, most of my problems were behind me, and a good and valuable friend of mine who struggles to believe in God was visiting with me and said, "Rod I have always had my doubts about God, but knowing the details of your story, and how it has all worked out, makes me believe you have a higher power watching out for you." He was exactly right. I totally believe that a higher power—God—rescued me!

I wrote this book for people who are driven to succeed. This story is for those who are leading companies, organizations, churches, schools, small businessses, or government agencies and are responsible for their success. Like me, most of these leaders have the best of intentions and put their heart and soul into their work. But any work that takes a person's focus away from God and their family, no matter how worthy the cause, will leave them unfulfilled and empty.

Anytime a committed leader of any cause is tirelessly working to accomplish that organization's goals, they will attract opposition and resistance. All organizations and endeavors require working closely with people, and anytime people are involved envy, jealously and pride will be present. Sadly, even in churches and not-for-profit causes, these conflicts occur. The temptations, troubles and problems that come with leadership are a heavy burden to bear. I tried to bear them alone, which led to my downfall. My prayer is that you can learn from my mistakes.

The story I am about to tell you has totally changed my life and strengthened my faith in God. I have a peace inside me that I never had before my troubles. I have a joy for living that I never had before my fall. I sure didn't deserve God's grace, because I was a huge hypocrite living a lie, but thankfully He sent his mercies into my life. First, He sent troubles to get my attention and then He sent caring guides to show me a better way to live. Finally, God saved me from all my troubles, took care of my needs, and answered all my prayers.

Why would I not want all my friends to have what I have found? When you find a treasure you want to share it. I have found something better than any treasure I have ever known and I want to share it with my friends.

If you have doubts about God, then read my story. If you want real peace and joy in your life, then read my story. If you're tired of struggling up each rung of the ladder of success only to find you're bitter at enemies, disappointed in friends and unfulfilled with victories, just ask God for help. Nothing can explain what happened to me except that God performed a miracle in my life and showed me a much better way to live. What He has done for me, He will do for you.

*"Success has ruined many a man."* – Benjamin Franklin

# Chapter 1
# "Don't Let This Place Change You"

S ession was over for the day, and I excitedly rushed out of my last committee meeting to attend a dinner party at the Hotel Deville, which many described as the nicest restaurant in Jefferson City. As a freshman representative in the minority, I hadn't yet been invited to many fancy dinners, and this was going to be my first visit to the Deville.

I had heard this was where the influential legislators hung out and by the time I arrived, the place was packed with all the powerful players from the capitol. As I walked, in I spotted several senators as well as prominent house chairmen already enjoying dinner with some of the top lobbyists and association directors in Missouri.

I felt fortunate to be included in a select group of freshmen legislators that the Cable Association asked a veteran Republican legislator to put together. They wanted to get to know some of the new faces, and the veteran was helping make the introductions.

To accommodate the large crowds that the legislative session brought in to the Deville, a round table had been set up in a spot not quite big enough for us to fit around. We worked our way into our seats at the cramped but elegant table and made the formal introductions. There were four freshmen, the veteran and three representatives from the Missouri Cable and Telecommunications Association (MCTA).

The veteran kept everyone entertained with stories about life in the capitol and the cable folks asked us new legislators basic questions about our political views, districts and families. When my turn came, I wanted to tell them about my thrilling campaign victory, but nobody seemed to care about campaigns in Jefferson City, so I stuck to the facts and told them about my conservative views, my family and Bollinger County. While the other freshmen were talking, I took some time to look around the room and watch the power brokers in action. There were very few lights in the Deville, which allowed the glimmering candle placed on each table to flicker and reflect off the crystal wine glasses and silver cutlery. The candle light also reflected in everyone's eyes when talking with them. Had I been there with my wife, it would have been very romantic, but with this crowd, it added a sinister tone to the dinner.

After the waiter brought drinks and took our orders, the veteran legislator joined the cable lobbyists in a fascinating conversation about what the session's priorities would be, what the new governor would do or how the senate leaders would respond, and a whole host of trifling legislative details that average citizens would find enormously tiresome. But our eager young legislative ears soaked up every word. Finding myself in the center of a city where laws and history were being made was thrilling. I was loving every minute of it as I sat there quietly strategizing about how I could some day advance my conservative agenda. I say "quietly" because I carefully followed the advice I'd been given earlier about listening and not talking as a freshman, but that didn't stop me from planning and scheming for the future.

Honestly, I hadn't been to many fancy restaurants in my lifetime before becoming a state representative. Growing up as a poor preacher's son, we rarely ate out and even when my real estate business was booming and I was making the "big" bucks, a fancy restaurant to me was Outback Steak House. Basically, any place that had a $15 entrée was expensive!

So to me, the Deville was a "fancy" restaurant with entrees that were $25 to $40. The menu that night included filet mignon, which even I knew was a nice steak. Since I was a teetotaler, I drank tea and ordered the filet. As the dinner continued and more wine was brought out, the conversation became livelier. I was careful to hold my tongue and only offered compliments about my peers and the veteran, as well as thanks to my hosts.

I was sitting next to Charlie Broomfield. He was a former democrat representative who lobbied for the MCTA. Charlie did more listening than talking and I don't think he drank much. But what he did at the end of this dinner is something I will never forget. As we were getting up to leave, former Representative Broomfield turned to me with a frightened look in his eye, put his hand on mine and squeezed it, as he said, "Don't let this place change you."

I had no idea what he was talking about and his hand, along with his look, startled me. As politely as possible, I pulled my hand away and assured him I would not change. Then I stood up, left the table and moved as far away from Charlie as I could. As a prideful freshman legislator, I had no fear about Jefferson City changing me. In fact, I was there specifically to change Jefferson City!

During my rise to Speaker of the House, I spent very little time thinking about Charlie Broomfield and what he said that night. But I have thought about it a lot since my political downfall. I don't know what he saw in me that made him decide to offer that very wise advice, because to my knowledge he didn't offer it to anyone else at the table. If only he would have pulled me aside and explained specifically what he was talking about or provided clear-cut examples... but he didn't. I doubt if an ambitious and successful kid like me would have listened even if he had.

Ambition and success are such problematic assets. They are filled with such good intentions. I had plenty of ambition and success seemed easy to obtain. To me everything about my life had been so easy... so honorable, but Charlie knew it wouldn't stay that way. He had been a powerful chairman working with other powerful leaders so he knew how ambition, success and power could change a person.

Unfortunately, I didn't heed the warning I didn't understand. And yes, I let "the place" change me. That is the most embarrassing admission about my failures. In the beginning it's hard for those with honest ambition to understand how success and power could ever change us. Regrettably, I learned firsthand that it can. In the pages that follow I'll attempt to illustrate to you the dangers of ambition and the hazards of power in an honest and understandable way. It's my prayer that reading about the experiences I've lived through will bear more fruit for you than Charlie's earnest advice did for me.

To share my story most effectively, let me take you back to the days long before fancy dinners and political talk. Back to a time when I was a young man with well-intentioned dreams of achieving great things. I hope you enjoy the journey.

# Chapter 2
# Christian Upbringing

*"Train up a child in the way that he should go and when he is old, he will not depart from it." – Proverbs 22:6*

My parents, Bill and Judy Jetton, raised me in a Christian home and taught me the difference between right and wrong. Not only did they teach me what was right, they lived it themselves. Many parents teach their kids one thing but do another. My parents did everything they taught me to do. I have never been able to blame my parents for my improper actions. They were the same in public as in private, an inspiration to us all.

I first realized I was a sinner and asked Jesus to forgive me of my sins when I was in the first grade. Then, when I was thirteen, I went forward in church one Sunday and recommitted myself to being a better Christian. After drinking and partying in my teenage years, I re-evaluated my lifestyle and with great difficulty stopped drinking. I again rededicated myself to a Christian life just before I was married at twenty years of age.

Like most of us, I struggled to do what was right as a

teenager. I was only having a good time with my friends. We never intended to hurt anyone, but a few of us ended up having trouble with drugs and alcohol. My Grandpa Jetton was an alcoholic, and during my teenage years my drinking was out of control. With the help of good counselors and many AA meetings, I finally quit, but it was extremely hard for me to stop drinking and get back on the right path. I deeply regretted my lifestyle and actions from fifteen to twenty years old.

Those first twenty years were marked by my efforts to live the life my parents taught me to live and the influence of foolish friends and selfish choices. The pursuit of pleasure and popularity caused me to fall far short of my good intentions.

I had faith that God was real and that He created the world we lived in, but I never heard His voice directly when I was growing up. I could only point to a few times where I even felt a clear direction as to what He wanted me to do.

I now see why I didn't feel His direction more. I spent very little time seeking His guidance. I rarely read the Bible and usually only prayed when I needed something. I had a temper and carried grudges, which separated me from God's will. Almost all my energies and efforts were for my personal ambitions. Like many young people, I was selfish. Along with being selfish, my adolescent successes in track, cross country, and student government planted those first seeds of pride that would prove damaging to me as I became an adult.

# Chapter 3
# Raising a Family

*"Many men can make a fortune, but very few can build a family." – J.S Bryan*

Just after my 21st birthday, during my junior year of college, I married Cassie James. She had a one-year-old daughter named Callie, whom I adopted. During the time I dated Cassie, I stopped drinking and made my spiritual walk with God more of a priority in my life. I had a new family and a new desire to learn a lot more about God and His commandments. I took my family to church, prayed for God's blessings, read my Bible, and paid my tithes. In those early years, God was faithful to answer my prayers and blessed me with another daughter, Emily, good health and financial rewards.

After graduating from college, I did a short stint in Congressman Bill Emerson's 1990 re-election campaign before joining the Marine Corps and moving to Jacksonville, North Carolina. We found a friendly church to attend with some wise Christian saints who helped me to better understand God's commandments. During this time the Lord answered my prayers and kept me safe in the Corps, and kept my family safe while I was overseas.

My son, Will, was born while I was in the Marine Corps, and soon after his birth I did a six-month overseas float. I was never involved in any real combat, but our unit did get pulled down off the coast of Somalia right after the Army Rangers were killed there. Marine life required me to be on training missions or overseas on security missions a lot. I missed so much of the kids growing up in those early years, but in the military, your life is not your own, as you have to follow orders.

Soon after returning to Marble Hill, Missouri, I started a real estate business with the help of my father-in-law, Frank James. Starting a new business was tough financially, and we didn't have health insurance during some of that time. Once again my prayers for good health and business success were answered. The company was very successful, and our family enjoyed perfect health. Once the company was up and running, I made my first foray into elected politics. In 1996, I ran for Bollinger County Commissioner and won my first campaign by 32 votes. At the age of 28, I was the youngest commissioner in the state.

During this time, my wife and I were active in our church in Marble Hill. My main job was teaching the young boys' class. Besides teaching them about the Bible, we took them camping and taught them how to live in the great outdoors. I took great pride in the fact that some of the boys made a decision to follow Christ under my teaching.

It was a very good time in my life. I joined the Optimist Club, was very active in church, and started each day by asking God to protect my family and bless my business. The Lord answered both of those prayers. I had a growing business, was respected in my community and most community leaders said I had turned out to be a "good" young man with a very bright future.

Up until this point, my story is very normal. A well-intentioned, hardworking young man graduates from high school, finds a good wife, starts a family, finishes college, serves in the military, starts a business, and is active in the betterment of his community. Many would say I messed it all up by going into politics, but I believe God opened the door for me to enter into politics.

# Chapter 4
# Headed to Jefferson City

*"Nothing is humbler than ambition, when it is about to climb."* – Benjamin Franklin

I was not new to the political world. Before joining the Marines I worked on Congressman Bill Emerson's campaign and I had managed Dan Meese's 1991, winning special election for Bollinger County sheriff. I was also a sitting county commissioner so I had some experience in the political world and thought myself a political genius.

I enjoyed a successful term as county commissioner serving with two experienced commissioners who taught me the ropes and helped me better understand what serving the public entailed. While I was in office we were able to keep taxes low and pay off a huge county debt, which watered the seeds of pride growing within me.

It wasn't long until the local state representative and other Republican leaders urged me to run for higher office. I was flattered and pleased at these overtures. What young man doesn't like hearing the praise of older and wiser men?

In 1999, State Representative Bill Foster announced he would not be running for re-election, which meant our community would be electing a new state representative. I received lots of encouragement to run, so I added this subject to my prayer list. I remember telling God that if He wanted me to run for office, He would have to send me some salespeople to help my real estate business.

My business was booming and there was no way I could take the time to run for office unless I got some help to keep up with all my customers. I had already been trying to find a salesperson to help but the search seemed useless. I don't know if it is best to tell God what to do, but the very week I asked for more salespeople I had two very capable men talk to me about working at my company (The two men are still successfully selling real estate today.).

Some would say it was just a coincidence, but it convinced me that I was supposed to run. I had told God that if He wanted me to run He had to send me help and after weeks of unsuccessfully looking for good salespeople, the week I prayed that prayer, I found two. Actually, I didn't find them, they approached me. I don't believe in coincidences, I believe in the providence of God. I truly felt the answer to my prayer was a signal for me to run for state representative.

I put all my energy into running for office while my hardworking wife and young family were there helping me each step of the way. I received lots of support, and our church friends were some of my best volunteers. I ended up winning a primary with 56 percent of the vote, and then cruised to a comfortable general election win.

I ran as a very conservative family values candidate determined to go to Jefferson City and reform Missouri. My slogan was "Fighting for Families," and I had no doubt about the righteousness of my cause. The big win and new position further cultivated the pride growing inside me.

My life was turning out almost like I planned it. Everything I wanted I got. While I had prayed for many of the blessings I received, I also worked hard. I lived by the rule, "Pray like it is all up to God, and work like it is all up to you." Unfortunately, I was starting to put more confidence in my work and less appreciation in God's help.

# Chapter 5
# Winning the Majority

*"I have always thought that one man of tolerable abilities may work great changes, and accomplish great affairs among mankind, if he first forms a good plan, and cutting off all amusements or other employments that would divert his attention, makes execution of that same plan his sole study and business." – Benjamin Franklin*

I didn't get much downtime after the November campaign in 2000. Right after Thanksgiving, the leaders wanted all of the new representatives in Jefferson City for three weeks of briefings. As a new representative, I found out about so many issues I never knew existed, and there was so much to learn about state government. I came home for Christmas, but my mind was already in another world talking to new friends about committee assignments, bill numbers, and legislative rules.

I couldn't wait for the session to start in January so I could begin implementing all of my good ideas, but once the 2001 session started, I received a sobering lesson in legislative politics. The Republicans were in the minority, and under the Missouri House rules, we had very little say in what laws were passed.

Most conservative bills were never even referred to a committee, and the few that were died there. We would then try to amend our conservative proposals to other bills during the floor debate, but the Democrats rarely allowed us to make an amendment, and the few times we did they easily voted us down because they had the majority. Many times we didn't even have the opportunity to debate bills and amendments, because the majority party would ignore us or end debate whenever they wanted.

I quickly wrote a detailed memo on how we could win the majority. I gave it to the minority leader, and she promptly appointed me the House Republican Campaign Committee (HRCC) chairman. This turned out to be a very important position in our caucus, because it set me up to be a key leader in the upcoming majority.

My HRCC position required me to recruit candidates to run for state representative in the 2002 campaigns. Term limits were forcing all of the old legislators out of office, and we believed this would give us a chance to win the majority. In Missouri, it took 82 seats for a majority and we already had 76. That year, there were 56 open seats where no incumbent would be running. If we could find good candidates, I felt we had a good chance of picking up the extra six seats we needed to win control of the chamber.

The Republicans had been in the minority for 48 years, so none of the political experts believed winning the majority was possible. Others before us had made plans, raised money, and recruited candidates only to fail. But our leader, Catherine Hanaway, and most of my fellow freshmen representatives rushed headlong into the effort, never considering that it couldn't be done.

We did find good candidates, and I trained them about how to win campaigns, while Catherine did a tremendous job of scraping together the money we would need to fund the races. Catherine and her chief of staff, Chuck Caisley, were the driving force behind our victory, but there were many other indispensable staff members, donors, and fellow representatives who helped us carry out the plan. As the election drew closer, even the old political experts started believing we just might pull it off. When the election results came in, we won race after race. Once they were all added up, we had a net gain of 14 districts, giving us 90 seats. For the first time in 48 years, the Republicans would have the majority and be in charge of the Missouri House.

The victory did not come without a personal cost for me. Once my first session was over in May 2001, I was on the road visiting most of the legislative districts in the state and meeting with prospective candidates. I normally came home on weekends, but there were many Friday night fundraisers that made that impossible. Missouri is a large state, and any trips to the northern or western side of the state usually kept me away for a couple of weeks.

Once session started in January, I was in Jefferson City all week and then taught campaign schools on the weekends or visited districts to assess the progress of the different campaigns. I was unopposed, so I didn't have to campaign at home, which kept me away from home over 230 days the year we won the majority in 2002.

Those first two years in the legislature were incredibly busy. I don't believe I have ever consistently worked that hard for that long at anything in my life, before or since. I thought working out twice each day and running a hundred miles a week in college was hard until I joined the Marine Corps and learned a new level of hard work. I was given ninety pounds of gear and ordered to march through the hills, with no rest or sleep, through all kinds of weather, for days on end. Then, after that, starting a small real estate business and making it profitable took early mornings and stressful nights, day in and day out.

But all those experiences were just preparing me for what it took physically, mentally and emotionally to recruit candidates, win the majority, unify caucus members, advance an agenda, get good press, and respond to donors all while trying to be a good father, loving husband, and solid community leader back home and in the district. Cassie was very understanding, but my time away from her and the kids would end up causing us problems.

# Chapter 6
# Elected to Leadership

*"Pray that success will not come any faster than you can endure it." – Elbert Hubbard*

Nobody knew all the new caucus members as well as I did. I had recruited them, trained them, slept on their couches and worked on their campaigns. When it came time to run for leadership positions in my party, I had most of the freshmen urging me to run. I was very supportive of Catherine serving as our Speaer, and she had counseled me to run for Speaker Pro-Tem, the number two position in the House. With her advice and the support of a huge freshmen class, I was elected unanimously.

In just two years, I went from being the lowest ranking member in the minority to Speaker Pro Tem of the Missouri House. It was very heady stuff. During my first two years, nobody cared what I thought and very few lobbyists stopped by my office. Suddenly everyone wanted to know what I thought about all kinds of issues, and there were lobbyists lined up outside my door waiting to talk with me about their pet project.

Our new Republican majority immediately introduced legislation to advance our conservative agenda. Some of the most conservative bills dealing with abortion and gun rights were vetoed by Governor Holden, but his vetoes only strengthened our commitment to generating change.

Catherine decided to run for Secretary of State, and my caucus unanimously elected me to take her place. It's hard to believe that after just four years in the House, I was Speaker. We did have an election to win before I could officially take over, so once again I traveled the state recruiting and training candidates, but in 2004 I also had to take on the fundraising duties.

Each election cycle I would help HRCC raise the $3.5 million we needed to keep the majority on top of raising thousands more for individual state representative candidates. As a campaign organizer, my reputation for fundraising, campaign strategy, message development, direct mail fundraising, and organizing grassroots efforts continued to grow. I started receiving more and more requests from candidates and party leaders to help others who were in tough races, which caused me to spend even less time at home with my family.

Republicans had not had a House Speaker in Missouri for 48 years, so it seemed every Republican county committee invited Catherine or me to be the keynote speaker for their annual Lincoln Day dinner. Caucus members all wanted me to be their special guest at their fundraisers, and numerous big donors and corporate leaders wanted to meet with me. It was very exciting and made me feel awfully important, so I rarely turned down an invitation.

I must have spoken to at least three dozen Lincoln Day audiences, attended over fifty fundraisers, and had over a hundred meetings with "important" Missouri leaders. Most of these meetings were not close to home in Southeast Missouri. Many required driving four to six hours away from home. It was a grueling pace, but I loved it! I was having a blast, everything was going my way, everyone loved me, respected me, and wanted to know what I thought about matters great and small. But between the speeches, fundraisers and meetings, I was home very little those next two years as well.

# Chapter 7
# Changing the State

*"I returned and saw under the sun, that the race is not to the swift, nor the battle to the strong, neither yet bread to the wise, nor yet riches to men of understanding, nor yet favor to men of skill; but time and chance happeneth to them all. – Ecclesiastes 9:11*

Most political observers agree that during the four years I was Speaker, we passed more major legislation changing Missouri than at any other time since Republicans have had the majority. It's important to remember it was the only four-year period in which Republicans had majorities in both legislative chambers and a Republican in the Governor's office. I do believe our aggressive new majority in the House was the catalyst for these changes, but without Governor Blunt signing our bills, we would not have been as successful.

I take some pride in what we were able to do in Missouri during those years. I'm pro-life, and we made it harder to get an abortion in our state, resulting in the lowest number of abortions performed in Missouri since 1975. I believe in the Second Amendment, and after several failed attempts by prior legislators in the 1990, we finally gave law-abiding citizens the right to carry a firearm.

In 2003, Missouri had a $1 billion deficit, but by the end of 2007 we had a $600 million surplus, and for the first time ever, we cut the size of our state work force by more than 3,000 employees. While our previous governor was forced to cut education funding because of the bleak budget situation, we were able to increase education funding by more than $500 million from 2005 to 2008.

Missouri also went from having the 47th worst roads in 2002 to the 9th best by 2007, resulting in 161 fewer deaths in 2006, which was the biggest drop of any state in America that year. Missouri went from being the No. 1 meth-producing state in America, with 2,860 meth incidents in 2003, to 1,280 in 2006. That's a 55 percent drop, which made our state a safer place to raise children.

Hopefully, my liberal friends have not stopped reading, because we also increased funding for "traditionally liberal" and meaningful programs such as autism support, S-CHIP's, Utilicare, First Steps, Meals on Wheels, food pantries and drug courts. Ironically, these are the same programs our Democrat governor and his Democrat majority were forced to cut in 2001 and 2002 when Missouri was going broke.

Another exciting aspect to this story was that our budget improved, and we increased funding for education and other vital programs with no new taxes.

In fact, we cut taxes. One of the few bills that I introduced and passed during my eight years was a tax cut on Social Security benefits.

Now, I certainly cannot take credit for all of this success, nor do I want to leave you with the impression that I am solely responsible for all of these changes. We had a unified team in the House pushing our agenda and a Republican majority in the Senate along with a friend in the Governor's office.

One other change I pushed for was a total overhaul of the House rules. I remembered what it was like to serve in the minority, and I led an effort to allow the minority more power to debate bills on the floor and in committee. Many in my party didn't like giving the minority more influence, but we mandated equal time to debate bills on the floor, allowed more time to read big bills before votes were taken, and passed several other provisions fostering constructive debate.

In the legislature, the majority has to keep the trains running on time and govern, but there is no reason why both sides of an issue shouldn't be debated. The minority sometimes just wants to stop everything, but our changes allowed them to make their points without shutting down the process. I made a big push to treat minority members with respect, which resulted in strong bipartisan votes on many of the bills that were passed and greatly improved relations between the parties. These changes led to more cooperation and compromise on many key issues, which was good for Missourians.

All in all, I believe things were better in Missouri because of the changes we were able to make, and I am thankful to have played a small part in changing the direction of our state. But there is a cost to everything, and while I was successful in the political world, I was quickly failing in the personal part of my life.

# Chapter 8
# Tangled up in the Cares of this World

*"Think of only three things: Your God, your family and the Green Bay Packers – in that order." – Vince Lombardi*

The pursuit of a goal is a worthy thing, and attaining any worthwhile goal takes discipline, focus and effort. My goal had been to make Missouri a better place to raise a family by passing a conservative agenda that included supporting traditional family values and slowing the growth of government. My liberal friends disagreed with me on how to make Missouri a better state, but we were both working toward the same goal. To change policy in a democracy, a person or party must gather power. It takes political power to change laws.

I was disciplined in the pursuit of my goal, and I brought a single-mindedness of purpose to the table. Unfortunately, I pushed everything in my life aside in the pursuit of accomplishing my goal. I was so consumed with climbing the political ladder and changing the state that I forgot what should have been the most important things in my life. While I was "fighting for families," I forgot about my family. My priorities were totally out of line. I should have listened to Coach Lombardi's advice above.

What I needed was balance. It's a simple word that makes the whole world go 'round. Balance is required for the sun, moon and stars to work like they do. It takes balance for us to walk, drive and function as humans. Most importantly, it takes balance to have healthy relationships with your spouse, kids, family, friends, co-workers and fellow citizens.

The biggest mistake I made was not having balance in my life. I worked too hard at politics and forgot about my family, faith, community and sometimes the whole reason I went to Jefferson City in the first place. I wish I could tell you when my pursuit of power and self-interest started becoming more important than making the state a better place, but I don't remember seeing a line in the sand.

I find most successful people deal with this same situation sometime in their lives. One day you're working hard, marching toward your worthy goals, helping others and providing for your family, before slowly second guessing the worthiness of your goals and wondering if anyone really appreciates your hard work.

I remember promising my wife, Cassie, that when the first campaign was over I would be home more. Then session started, and I promised that after session I would be home more. Then I was gone working on redistricting and when that was finished the next session had started and after that I was working night and day to win the majority, but I promised her that once we won, this time I would be home.

I didn't realize winning the majority would take even more of my time or that everyone would be depending on me and I would become even more entangled in my political life. The few times she complained, I thought she should have understood I had more important things to do besides mow the grass, attend games, go to teacher conferences or hang out with her. I mean, we were trying to change the state, and I was making things better and passing all the issues we believed in. The fact is I was working on good things, but she was all alone raising three kids who never saw their dad. Unfortunately, my actions proved that work was more important than them, no matter what I said.

You're probably wondering how I could have been so stupid. I don't want to make excuses, but I compared my political responsibilities and traveling around the state to my time in the Marine Corps serving overseas. In my mind, the Marine Corps was even harder because you left for six months and never came home. At least in politics I was home each week.

In hindsight, I can see why Cassie was upset. In the Marine Corps, I had no choice and there was always a date when she knew I would be home from deployment or finishing my time on active duty. In politics I kept moving the date back, or adding one more hurdle, and making one more empty promise. She was patient at first, but after a few years of broken promises, she felt unloved.

There were other changes and other misplaced priorities in my life during this time. In Chapter 3, I mentioned how I started each day with prayer and asked God to bless my efforts and my family. Unfortunately, my life in politics left little time for praying. I stayed up late at night working and got up early to tackle the next day's to-do list. When I first ran for state representative, I would say a quick prayer over each fundraising letter I sent and each speech I gave. I remember praying, "Dear God, please let them send a donation in, or let me have a clear mind as I speak." As I became more successful, I forgot how God had answered my prayers, and became more focused on how hard I had worked.

Most of my troubles began when I started depending on myself instead of God. I no longer started each day asking God to protect my family and bless my efforts. Instead, each morning I woke up with a long to-do list that didn't leave any time for prayer, and each night I was too tired to take time to pray before falling asleep. The lack of prayer to protect my family led to troubles on the home front, and in my experience, once a person has troubles at home they will soon have troubles in their professional life. For me, it was like falling dominos. First, my spiritual life was pushed aside, which led to problems at home and those problems led to troubles at work.

I also stopped attending church. Oh, I always went on Sunday morning because I had to keep up appearances. Then after church I would come home, take a nap and then head to Jefferson City to "save" the state. Before I ran for representative, I attended both Sunday and Wednesday night services. But once I became "important," I was just too busy to go on those nights. I thought I needed to be in Jefferson City on Sunday night to be prepared for Monday, and there were always meetings or events in Jefferson City on Wednesday night. Even during the Sunday morning service I was not thinking about God. Instead, I spent most of the service checking my phone and sending text messages.

As a "family values" politician, I needed to go to church, but I was drifting slowly away from the Lord. All the responsibility, flattery and important things I was working on caused me to become very prideful. I was growing less dependent on God and much more dependent on myself.

I knew I needed to pray more and even bought some Bible study books with the intention of getting back on track, but each time I tried, it seemed that some "emergency" would come up and I would put prayer, Bible study and church off.

I also started to believe that I was indispensable to Missouri politics, and helping everyone else left me too busy to ask for God's help. Besides drifting away from my faith and pushing my family to the back burner, I made one other major mistake that led to even more problems. I started drinking again.

Why was I willing to do something that had caused me so many problems and been so hard to quit when I was younger? Even though drinking was a major problem for me as a young man, somehow time and success had clouded my memory. You may be thinking, "Politics is a dirty business, Rod, and you have to drink to move up," but that's not true. I quickly rose through the ranks all the way to Speaker without drinking. Legislators, lobbyists and donors all knew I didn't drink. In fact, not drinking was an advantage because I was able to learn a lot from those who drank too much and told every secret they knew while not saying anything stupid myself.

The problems that drinking had caused me as a teenager seemed to fade from my memory by the time I was in my thirties. As I drifted away from my faith, the pressures that come with a powerful office along with problems at home started taking their toll, and I thought a drink would help me relax. At first I only drank a beer or two in my office after stressful days. Then I started sharing a few drinks over dinner with trusted allies, but it wasn't long before I looked forward to relaxing with a few drinks each night.

Now I am not trying to say drinking makes you a bad person or sends you to Hell. We know Jesus turned the water into wine, and there is no verse in the Bible that says you cannot drink. However, there are several verses that tell us not to get drunk. We all know that if you drink you will eventually get drunk. Nobody limits themselves to just a couple of drinks forever. Eventually you have too much wine or too many beers and lose your judgment. My dad, who grew up in the home of an alcoholic father always said, "Drinking causes a lot more bad than good." That has sure been true in my life.

For me, drinking was the wrong decision. It impaired my judgment and caused me to make more bad decisions. I also tried to hide my drinking from my kids, parents, friends back home, and church leaders around the state. Living a double life and being a hypocrite was hard on me mentally. Somehow during those first four years as a state representative, my goal of making Missouri a better state was ruining my life.

Somewhere along the way my desire for prominence, power and popularity took over as my driving force. I didn't realize this was happening, and I still believed I was fighting for my original policy goals. I even passed most of the laws I had first campaigned on, but for me the legislative and political process was starting to be more about personal wins or losses and less about what I was changing.

# Chapter 8
# Pride, Bitterness and Becoming Paranoid

*"The crucible is for refining silver and the smelter for gold, but a person is tested by the praise given to him." –* Proverbs 27:21, GOD'S WORD

The whole time that my personal life was quietly spiraling out of control, my political success was spiraling up, gaining me accolades from friends and criticism from opponents. Now success and accolades can be wonderful things, but if you're not careful, success can kill you. It sure took a toll on me. I tried to hide my vanity and pride, but deep down in my mind, I started to believe all the things lobbyists, other members, donors and conservative activists were saying about me.

As a public official with power over funding and other members' bills, as well as all the laws people live by, folks tended to tell me what I wanted to hear. Everyone told me what a good job I was doing, how smart I was, how thankful they were that I was in charge ... or that nobody else had ever done it as well as I had.

Of course, in politics not everyone was singing my praises. In Missouri, the *Kansas City Star* and *St. Louis Post-Dispatch* were not very friendly to a conservative Republican like me. My political work helping friends who wanted to move up to the State Senate or U.S. Congress caused the press to endlessly attack me. Liberals and those opposed to my agenda sent me thousands of e-mails and letters that sometimes were just plain mean. Running Mitt Romney's Missouri presidential race in 2008 didn't make me many friends either.

Between my political activities, legislative duties and outspoken tell-it-like-it-is attitude, I started picking up quite a few new enemies, and they never hesitated to start a nasty rumor or provide a negative quote about me when they could. Oddly enough, most of my attacks came from fellow Republicans.

Because of all of the criticism, I made the mistake of totally tuning out my critics. Letting your critics get you down is something you have to avoid, but paying attention to their criticisms and considering that they often have a point is one good way to improve your weaknesses.

At times, I have found that my opponents have done the best job of candidly pointing out my weaknesses. Too often in life, I didn't realize that fact until after my weaknesses caused me problems.

You are probably asking why I didn't listen to my critics, or at least think about their charges. Well, people said such terrible things about me as a politician and my motives were constantly being mischaracterized that I developed a very thick skin. For me it was easy to chalk up all of their negative comments and criticism to the idea that they were enemy hacks who hated me because I was either beating them in the legislative chess game or defeating them on the campaign trail. I told myself that no matter what I did they would complain. My experience has shown me how easy it is for powerful leaders to listen to the flattery and discount their critics when they are under fire.

Another negative consequence of the simultaneous flattery and criticism was that I started putting everyone into one of two camps. People were either for me or against me, and if anyone was critiquing me or even questioning me, I decided they must be against me. I became paranoid when friends or neutral folks, who were just being honest, tried to tell me the truth. The longer I was in power the more this happened, and it affected several of my relationships.

But let's get back to the flattery. It slowly started affecting me. Not in the beginning. I knew what they were doing, and I told myself not to pay attention to them. But flattery has a way of slowly creeping in and changing a person's attitude. At least it did mine.

Have you ever heard the story about the frog that was placed in the pot of boiling water and immediately jumped out and survived? If you have, then you know that same frog didn't fare so well when he was placed in some cold water while the heat was slowly turned up until he was boiled to death and never even knew it. It's very embarrassing to admit that this happened to me. Looking back on my time in the legislature, I feel a bit like the frog that was slowly cooked to death and just didn't feel the heat rising. In fact, the warm water feels kind of good after a while.

As a powerful Speaker, I was in a pot of boiling water and didn't even know it. My pride had blinded me to my problems. I became a very bitter person. My marriage was in terrible shape, and I was mad at my wife. I blamed all of our problems on her, and pride blinded me from seeing my own faults. My political enemies were continually attacking me, so I woke up each morning wondering who was trying to kill me, ready to take them out first.

Anytime anyone stood in the way of what I thought needed to be accomplished, I was ready and willing to do whatever it took to get them out of the way. The anger and bitterness I felt for my opponents was clouding my judgment and affecting my friendships.

Pride not only blinded me to my own weaknesses but caused me to underestimate obstacles and often the strengths of my opponents. Once I lost my perspective on those things, I was headed for a fall. With my judgment impaired, mistakes quickly followed. My prideful attitude was attracting conflict, strife, and discord with those around me, while at the same time repelling trust, friendship, and loyalty.

The bitterness and pride clouded my ability to effectively read people and assess the situation. I would quickly mistrust almost anyone who questioned my goals, strategies or methods. My circle of trusted friends kept shrinking, because I repelled well-meaning allies who were only giving me their honest opinion.

I was not one of those loudmouth, commanding leaders yelling at people all the time. I used every trick I knew to get people to willingly go along with my plans. I stayed respectful of others but quietly behind the scenes I moved the chess pieces where I wanted them. I cut deals and did favors to accomplish my goals. I started believing that the ends justify the means.

Now I don't want to leave the impression that I was a mean guy walking the halls looking for fights. I won my Speaker race because I was a nice guy and helped others, but as Speaker fights came looking for me. Each day I had to make tough decisions and each decision usually made somebody happy and somebody mad. Sometimes the hard decisions leave a lot of people angry and only a few happy. I learned that the ones who were mad never forgot about it and the ones who were happy seemed to have short memories. I started out as a caring, helpful, happy-go-lucky guy, but I let the fights take away my optimistic attitude, and I slowly grew less caring, less helpful, and less happy with my life.

I didn't become bitter overnight. It took time. I had people do terrible things to me. I was double-crossed, sold out, and stabbed in the back. Sometimes even my good friends, or those I loved, hurt me. Rejection and betrayal by those you depend on the most is the fastest way to become bitter and paranoid. I have found that my enemies never hurt me as much as my friends and allies did. I expected my enemies to try hurting me, but I thought I could trust my friends.

What I should have done when these first "troubles" hit was get on my knees and ask the Lord to help me. Unfortunately, I thought I could handle it myself. I had drifted away from God, so when my problems came and friends betrayed me I started making plans to "fix" things myself.

I looked at it like combat and decided that if they threw a punch, I would pull a knife, or if they pulled a knife, I would bring a gun. During those first four years, I didn't start any fights, but I definitely didn't turn the other cheek. It didn't take me long to build up a list of enemies, and I aggressively went after them.

In the House, it takes a united team to change things. Developing an agenda, unifying our caucus behind it, and leading them in the public debate was a very worthwhile experience that required using the carrot and the stick. I rewarded both Democrat and Republican friends alike. I helped them with their priorities and gained their support on our agenda. But I also punished my opponents.

I made it clear that if you crossed my allies or me, there would be consequences. I removed chairmen, kicked members out of their offices, disregarded senators' bills, and ignored the Governor's priorities, with no regard for party affiliation. In my mind, you were either helping my caucus pass our priorities or you were slowing us down.

At first these fights were principled and brought me allies and friends, but as time passed and my bitterness grew, my fights were less about principles and more about my pride and the act of winning. There is an old saying in politics, "Friends come and go while enemies accumulate." For me, the enemies were accumulating quickly.

# Chapter 10
# Heading for a Fall

*"Pride goeth before destruction and a haughty spirit before a fall." – Proverbs, 16:18*

I was not a happy person during my last term as Speaker. I should have been enjoying everything I had accomplished politically, but my bitterness toward my opponents and family problems at home dominated my thoughts. Officially, I was a political success. Like most legislative leaders, I received award after award from almost every trade association in Missouri, and several political experts named me as one of the most powerful politicians in the state. My name was even on a short list to run for Governor in 2008.

Privately, all I wanted was to get out of elected office. My marriage was in bad shape and headed for divorce. I was tired of getting beat up in the press, tired of worrying about my enemies taking me out, and tired of feeling responsible for all the problems that needed fixing in our state. I left office at the end of 2008 and thought that as a private citizen doing campaign consulting, I would be able to stay behind the scenes, work on my friends' campaigns and not be in the crosshairs each and every day.

My drinking was clouding my judgment, and there were a few instances when I cheated on my wife that last year. I had a few close friends, some caring staff members, and a couple of brave lobbyists advise me to straighten up and get back on the right path, but I didn't listen. I just let my bitterness, hurt and anger control me.

In early 2009, my wife and I separated and by that October we were divorced. I tried to tell everyone that it was a good thing for me, but inside I hurt. After all, we had been married almost twenty years and were nearly finished raising three wonderful kids. Despite my mistakes, I still loved her.

I headed out of office as a 42-year-old successful divorced man, whose personal life was not turning out like I had planned. My dad was a Baptist preacher, and the best parents in the world had given me a perfect childhood. I was a family values conservative Republican who was not supposed to have these types of problems. My life was not reflecting the values my parents had taught me, nor was I being the example I wanted my kids to see.

Though leaving office and being divorced left me feeling free, I made the same mistake many divorced people make. I went looking for love in all the wrong places. I hit the bars and monitored Match.com looking for possible dates. I went out with a lot of girls and lived a very immoral lifestyle. I was running a successful consulting company during the day, but each night was all about partying with women and drinking.

I rented a nice apartment in St. Louis and lived the "high life" with all the other divorced people who were looking for love. There were plenty of women who were mad at their exes, didn't want to get married again, and felt that they were finally free to have fun. Sadly, in America today, there are too many angry divorced people hanging out at the bars and hooking up with other angry divorcees trying to drown their sorrows or forget their emotional pain. Unfortunately, they are only hurting themselves, their children and causing a lot more pain.

Even while I was living the wild life, at the end of the day, when I was all by myself, I found it very unfulfilling. As the old saying goes, "The grass is always greener on the other side." It was fun for a while, but soon I found myself missing my wife. I missed my kids, I missed our home, but I tried to get those thoughts out of my mind by drinking and partying even more.

I tried to stop drinking. I was scheduled to run the Marine Corps marathon that October, and I told myself I needed to quit drinking for 30 days before the race. I tried and even went a week or so before taking a drink. I didn't tell anyone, but I knew then that my old problem was back and decided I would try to quit again after the race.

Sadly, I was still trying to keep this wild lifestyle hidden from my family. Even though I am not Catholic,

I attended the Catholic Church that was near my apartment. I remember spending a lot of time justifying my lifestyle. I knew it was wrong, but I told myself we are all sinners and since God forgives sinners, He surely would forgive me. I went to Mass almost every Sunday and between emails and texts I prayed for forgiveness, before heading out for another week of partying.

That was how 2009 went for me. Working each day, drinking each night and constantly looking for a lady to have fun with. Finally, in December 2009, God had enough of my immoral ways and got my attention. After spending the night with a lady I had reconnected with on Facebook, I was charged with felony assault.

# Chapter 11
# Breaking One Last Promise

*"When you make a promise to God, don't be slow to keep it because God doesn't like fools. Keep your promise. It is better not to make a promise than to make one and not keep it." – Ecclesiastes 5:4-5 GOD'S WORD*

It was supposed to just be a fun night of sex. We had texted each other with requests and talked about some wild rough sex. We even agreed to a safe word to make sure nothing went too far. I went to her house, engaged in some basic chitchat, watched some TV, drank a glass of wine, and then got down to the reason I had shown up. I woke up and spent the next morning getting some work done on my laptop at her house. We made plans for dinner later that week; I gave her a kiss goodbye, and then left at around 11 a.m.

There was nobody more surprised than me when five days later I received a call from a Missouri Highway Patrol officer. The officer left me a message saying he wanted to ask me a few questions about the night of

November 15. I was shocked. I tried to call the lady and ask what was the matter but couldn't get an answer. I also received a call from one of her friends promising to ruin my life, and I slowly started understanding what was happening.

I called a lawyer to ask what I should do. I told him the basic facts of the story, and he agreed to call the Highway Patrol officer and get more information. I was scared and extremely worried about this getting out into the public. I quickly got on my knees and begged God to help me, while I promised to stop drinking and running around with women.

My lawyer reported back that after looking into the case more and learning of the agreed safe word, the Highway Patrol didn't think there was a reason to move forward and didn't need to talk with me. I let out a sigh of relief and thought my troubles were over. I went through Thanksgiving thinking everything was fine and quickly forgot about my prayer and promise to God.

Then, I broke my promise the first week in December when I agreed to meet a lady at a bar. After several drinks, we headed back to my apartment, and I did exactly what I had promised God I would not do if he helped me out of my troubles.

It didn't take long for the details about my evening to spread through Missouri political circles. I was worried but felt I could deny it and keep it quiet. I didn't know it, but after the Highway Patrol dropped the investigation, the local police department decided to pick it up. On December 7, I was sitting in my office in Jefferson City when I received a phone call from a friend letting me know there was a warrant out for my arrest. I found out just in time to slip out the back door of my office before the cameras and press showed up.

I didn't know what to do. My secret immoral life was about to be exposed, and the only thing I could think about was what I would tell my parents and kids. I have never in all my life given any serious thought to suicide, but for just a moment, before the public learned about my secrets, I considered that my family would be better off if I was dead. I knew my insurance policy would take care of the kids, and I thought my death might lessen their embarrassment.

I quickly put those thoughts out of my mind but still didn't know what to do. I had been in some high-pressure situations in politics and the Marine Corps, but nothing had prepared me for this kind of crisis. My mind raced as to how to handle this situation.

The thing I dreaded most was calling my dad. My dad is the best Christian man I know. I have never heard him say a cuss word and he has always lived the Christian life he taught. Dad was always very strict, and there was never any grey area with him; everything was either right or wrong. He always raised me to be tough. Mercy and compassion were not things he stressed.

Dad is also a preacher, and he was working with about 30 churches in southeast Missouri in 2009. Having a son accused of assaulting a woman during rough sex would not be well received in the religious community. I didn't want to call him, but I knew he was going to find out. I felt I needed to let him know what was going to happen, and I had no one else to call.

While dodging the press, I called him standing outside of the bail bondsman's office. He answered, and I told him there was a warrant out for my arrest and I was getting ready to turn myself in. Of course, this surprised him and not knowing the details he was a bit confused, so I explained that I had been living a very wicked life and had a one-night stand with a woman who was accusing me of assault, and I was going to jail. I went through some of the details and told him the radio, TV and newspapers would soon be saturated with my photo and the sordid details of the accusations.

Once dad understood the situation, he did something I never expected him to do. He said, "Son, I hate that this is happening to you, and I do not approve of your activities, but I love you no matter what." Wow! A father's love is amazing. I love my dad so much, and he is such a good dad and a good man who always seems to do the right thing. While he was serving the Lord, I was doing everything he was against, but he still loved me!

I thank the Lord that my dad loved me when he should have hated me. He explained everything to mom and right there on the phone they prayed for me. They prayed that God would use this situation to help me get my life back on track. What a mom and dad! I don't deserve them, and they sure did not deserve a son like me.

Once the press couldn't find me at my office, they came to my apartment. I hid inside and didn't answer the door. Around midnight, when I thought the press would not be expecting me, I snuck over to the sheriff's office and turned myself in. I remember feeling unbearably alone when the door to that jail slammed behind me.

They took my mug shot, fingerprints, all my possessions and I had to sign several forms and answer many questions. To the deputies, it was just a normal administrative process, but to me it seemed like my life was over. I sat there looking at the other prisoners wondering how it had come to this. The whole process seemed like a dream. I kept thinking I would wake up and it would be over, but I didn't and it wasn't.

Jail is a cold, hard, dirty place. Everything is either concrete or metal and all the metal is painted grey. There were no blankets, cushions or carpet. It wasn't comfortable, it wasn't warm, and nobody was friendly. It seemed like it took forever to finish all of the paperwork. I was fortunate that all I had to do was turn myself in, get processed, and wait for my bondsman to bail me out. I can't remember how long it took, but I was very tired when they opened the door and let me back out.

Thankfully, there were no cameras to greet me as I shuffled out into the cold morning air. I quickly walked back to my apartment, which was only two blocks away and tried to go to sleep, but sleeping didn't come easy. The next day I shut down my political consulting business and spent the next week avoiding the press by hiding in my apartment and refusing to answer the door.

# Chapter 12
# Three Chances to Change

*"And the Lord turned, and looked on Peter. And Peter remembered the word of the Lord, how he had said unto him, Before the cock crows, thou shalt deny me thrice. And Peter went out and wept bitterly." – Luke 22:61-62*

That night, before I fell asleep, I read my Bible. Dad had always told me to read a chapter of Proverbs each day, but it had been a long time since I had done it. There are 31 chapters in Proverbs, which is one for each day in most months. On December 7, I opened my Bible and started reading Proverbs seven. Ironically, Proverbs seven talks about a man who chases after women and the conclusion of his immoral ways ends in destruction. I remembered reading that proverb when I was younger, but it had been years since I had thought about it. I was sure thinking about it that night, and like Peter after his denial of Christ, I wept bitterly.

That night started a week of reading my Bible, crying out to God for forgiveness and repenting of my sins. I also read a book my mother had given to me years before, which I had never even opened, Andrew Murray's The Deeper Christian Life. The more I read my Bible and Murray's writings, the worse I felt about all the sinful things I had done.

All the times over the last four years I had been to church, all the times I felt bad for my sins, and all the times I had promised God I would do better, came rushing back to me. I never shed a tear during those encounters; I never opened my Bible or read God's word. I had felt guilt, I had felt regret, and I sure wanted help with my problems, but I never truly felt sorry enough to repent of my sins.

Sometimes troubles seem to be the only way God can get my attention. Why is that? Why did it take me almost destroying my life to make me realize I needed to change my ways? I do not know the answer to that question. I know God gave me many opportunities to change my ways. I distinctly remember God giving me three major chances to change my ways before my world came crashing down that December night.

In the spring of 2006, I sat in Harmony Church in Marble Hill, Missouri, and our pastor, Bro. Ross, preached a Sunday sermon on Peter's denial. I don't remember all the particulars, but I remember when he gave the invitation and invited us to come forward, I knew I needed to go forward, get on my knees, turn my life around, and ask for forgiveness. I grabbed the pew as hard as I could and resisted making that decision.

I stood there and told myself, "What will other church members think? I'm an important state representative who is a Christian, and if I go up now, everyone will wonder what's wrong with me." I also wondered how I would stop hanging out with my friends who were drinking and partying. I was having fun and didn't think I could just drop those activities. My life had not spiraled out of control at that point, but it was headed that way. I believe I could have saved myself a lot of trouble had I turned my life around that day in Marble Hill.

The second time I clearly felt God pulling me toward repentance was later that year listening to Christian apologist, Ravi Zacharias, on the radio while driving to Jefferson City. Again, I do not remember his sermon, but I remember thinking I needed to get back on track and turn things around. When I got to Jefferson City, I ordered an audio Bible study called Experiencing God, and planned on listening to it but was so busy I never even opened it.

After that, my moral life went downhill rather quickly. It's hard to hear from God while you're running away from Him. Then right before my world blew up, I believe He gave me one more chance to turn from my wicked ways, but I threw away that opportunity as well. I already mentioned my "foxhole confession" once I learned the police were looking into the assault accusations. I believe that was my last chance to humble myself, ask for forgiveness and turn from my wicked ways. My logic and life were so twisted at that point that I flat out lied to God. I made him a promise that I promptly broke, and he allowed me to be tangled up in my own net of hypocrisy and deceit.

# Chapter 13
# King Manasseh

*"This is a faithful saying, and worthy of all acceptance, that Christ Jesus came into the world to save sinners, of whom I am chief." – 1st Timothy 1:15*

I spent most of my time the first few weeks after my arrest praying and reading my Bible. The more I read the worse I felt about my actions. My eyes were opened to how far I had wandered from God. I felt then and still feel today like I am one of the worst sinners in history. I have known bad people in my life, and I've read about David, Paul and Peter's mistakes in the Bible, but I felt like I had made more mistakes than any of them.

I had great parents who taught me God's commandments and the right way to live. Plus, I had been a prodigal son as a teenager and strayed from God, but He helped me to stop drinking and get back on the right path. Over the years, God had blessed me with a healthy family and successful business. After all that, why would I doubt God or drift away from Him? I could not claim ignorance; I couldn't say I didn't understand.

It was willful disobedience and I knew better.

My business partner, Eric Brooks, was a good Christian man, and he knew my life was spiraling out of control. Still, he kept our business going strong. When I was arrested, he helped me close the company down and sort things out. Eric was so kind, even though my actions negatively affected his job and our company.

Eric told me about a Bible character I was not very familiar with. He said there was a king in Judah named Manasseh who was the most wicked king in Judah's history. While he was king, the Assyrians captured Jerusalem and put Manasseh in chains and took him back to Babylon. Once in captivity, Manasseh repented of his sins and asked God for forgiveness. God heard his prayer and restored him to his throne in Jerusalem. It is recorded this way in 2 Chronicles 33:11-13 "Wherefore the LORD brought upon them the captains of the host of the king of Assyria, which took Manasseh among the thorns, and bound him with fetters, and carried him to Babylon. And when he was in affliction, he besought the LORD his God, and humbled himself greatly before the God of his fathers, and prayed unto him: and he was intreated of him, and heard his supplication, and brought him again to Jerusalem into his kingdom. Then Manasseh knew that the LORD, he was God."

After hearing his story I spent a lot of time learning about King Manasseh. His father, King Hezekiah, was one of the most godly kings in Judah's history. He stopped all idol worship and put the priests back in charge of the temple and reinstituted the Passover sacrifices. The Lord blessed him with wealth and Hezekiah defeated all of his enemies. He became sick in his old age, and after the prophet Isaiah told him to get his house in order because he would die, Hezekiah prayed to the Lord and asked to recover from his sickness. Because of his faithfulness, God answered his prayer and sent Isaiah to tell him that the Lord would heal him and give him fifteen more years. God even gave Hezekiah a sign that he would be healed by moving the sun backward ten degrees.

Hezekiah's son, Manasseh, was the longest reigning king in Jewish history. He ruled for 55 years. Despite having a Godly father who removed idol worship from Judah, Manasseh put the altars of Baalim back up in Judah and even worshiped other false gods in the Lord's temple. He also sacrificed his children by fire, practiced sorcery, and consulted wizards. The Bible says he was more wicked than all the other kings before him. 2 Kings 21:16 says, "Moreover, Manasseh shed innocent blood very much, till he had filled Jerusalem from one end to another; beside his sin by which he made Judah to sin, in doing evil in the sight of the Lord."

I felt I was probably a lot like King Manasseh. I had a Godly father who followed all the Lord's commands and taught me to follow them, yet I still failed. I turned away from those teachings and did the exact opposite of what I was taught. Like Manasseh, God was tired of my wicked lifestyle and troubles came upon me. While

I was not in captivity, everything I thought was important was gone. Money, power, reputation and prominence were all gone. Thankfully, I still had my family and health.

King Manasseh's prayer is not in the King James Bible, but it is recorded in ancient Jewish writings. I looked it up and read it for myself. This is from the Codex Alexandrinus a fifth century manuscript of the Greek Bible:

*1 O Lord Almighty,*
*God of our ancestors,*
*of Abraham and Isaac and Jacob*
*and of their righteous offspring;*
*2 you who made heaven and earth*
*with all their order;*
*3 who shackled the sea by your word of command,*
*who confined the deep*
*and sealed it with your terrible and glorious name;*
*4 at whom all things shudder,*
*and tremble before your power,*
*5 for your glorious splendor cannot be borne,*
*and the wrath of your threat to sinners is*
*unendurable;*
*6 yet immeasurable and unsearchable*
*is your promised mercy,*
*7 for you are the Lord Most High,*
*of great compassion, long-suffering, and very*
*merciful,*
*and you relent at human suffering.*

*O Lord, according to your great goodness*
*you have promised repentance and forgiveness*
*to those who have sinned against you,*
*and in the multitude of your mercies*
*you have appointed repentance for sinners,*
*so that they may be saved.*
*8 Therefore you, O Lord, God of the righteous,*
*have not appointed repentance for the righteous,*
*for Abraham and Isaac and Jacob, who did not sin*
*against you,*
*but you have appointed repentance for me, who am a*
*sinner.*
*9 For the sins I have committed are more in number*
*than the sand of the sea;*
*my transgressions are multiplied, O Lord, they are*
*multiplied!*
*I am not worthy to look up and see the height of*
*heaven*
*because of the multitude of my iniquities.*
*10 I am weighted down with many an iron fetter,*
*so that I am rejected because of my sins,*
*and I have no relief;*
*for I have provoked your wrath*
*and have done what is evil in your sight,*
*setting up abominations and multiplying offenses.*
*11 And now I bend the knee of my heart,*
*imploring you for your kindness.*
*12 I have sinned, O Lord, I have sinned,*
*and I acknowledge my transgressions.*
*13 I earnestly implore you,*

*forgive me, O Lord, forgive me!*
*Do not destroy me with my transgressions!*
*Do not be angry with me forever or store up evil for*
me;
    *do not condemn me to the depths of the earth.*
    *For you, O Lord, are the God of those who repent,*
    *14 and in me you will manifest your goodness;*
    *for, unworthy as I am, you will save me according to*
your great mercy,
    *15 and I will praise you continually all the days of my*
life.
    *For all the host of heaven sings your praise,*
    *and yours is the glory forever. Amen.*

This prayer is a lot like David's prayer of repentance in Psalms 51. In both prayers the petitioners acknowledges their sins and trouble, ask God for forgiveness and pledge to give God praise if He will deliver them from their troubles. David added this line about transgressors in verse 13, "Then I will teach transgressors thy ways, and sinners shall be converted." I thought about Manasseh and David, and believed that if God could forgive them, He would forgive me, too.

I prayed a similar prayer by acknowledging my sins and troubles. I begged the Lord for forgiveness and promised God I would give Him praise if He would save me from my troubles. I also pledged to do all I could to help others avoid my mistakes.

I cannot describe the freedom confession provided

me. I felt a peace that I had not felt in years. Those days alone in my apartment were precious, but my confession and God's forgiveness did not mean He was done working on me. I would soon learn that my actions had consequences, and that reaping what I had sown would not be easy.

# Chapter 14
# Ruining the Family Name

*"A good name is rather to be chosen than great riches, and loving favor rather than silver and gold." – Proverbs 22:1*

When I finally ventured out of my apartment I drove to Southeast Missouri and spent some time with my parents and children talking about my mistakes. They had many questions, and I tried to answer them and apologize for all the trouble I had caused. My dad even considered resigning from his position with the Cape Girardeau Baptist Association.

Those were some very hard conversations. It was not easy telling my children about my double life. I had to explain why I had done all the things I taught them not to do. My heart overflowed with a sense of failure and regret as I saw the disappointment in their eyes. Yet I will forever be so very thankful for their love. I had put them on the back burner and pushed my family aside for my professional glory. When my power and prestige were gone the only thing that I had left was my family and, thankfully, they still loved me.

There was no way to sugarcoat my mistakes. I couldn't blame it on political enemies or ignorance. It was all my fault, and despite all the trouble I was causing them, they still loved me. It brings tears to my eyes each time I think about how loving Callie, Emily, Will, mom and dad were to me in that situation.

While I knew my story was in the press, I really didn't understand how bad things had gotten. I had quickly made the decision to shut down my political consulting business and save my clients as much embarrassment as possible. The immoral nature of the accusations made working for conservative Republicans impossible, and I very much regretted causing them problems.

I didn't know what to do for work so I called Sam Licklider, who was the lobbyist for the Missouri Realtors Association and had always been fair to me. He was kind enough to take my call and I asked him if he knew of any Realtors around the Lake of the Ozarks who might be willing to take me on as a salesman. I told him that around the lake I probably wouldn't be recognized.

He chuckled and said, "Rod, there is no place in this state where you will not be recognized. This story has been all over the press and everyone is talking about it." He agreed to check with a few people and called me back a few days later with a name. I will always be appreciative of his kindness in those dark days.

My son, Will, was very upset because several boys at school had been giving him a hard time about me and my problems. He was playing on the Woodland High School basketball team, and Cassie along with some other friends were very concerned about me even showing up to watch his games. They were worried someone might confront me and it would cause a scene.

Within those first few weeks, all of Missouri's major newspapers and most TV and radio stations had run multiple stories about my case. In Southeast Missouri it was even worse. I was the top story on the main TV station each morning, noon and evening for almost three weeks. They even came to Marble Hill to ask folks what they thought about the scandal. They continually repeated the accusations that I had drugged, beaten and assaulted a defenseless woman. It was not a positive story, and there was not much I could do to fight or counter the charges. I had been with the woman, we did have rough sex, and while I believed our experience was consensual, my attorney told me to save my response for court.

I did receive some very good advice from a gentleman who had been accused of some serious and negative accusations of which he was eventually found not guilty. He told me I needed to get back out in the public and go about normal life. He said, "I understand that you are embarrassed and wonder what people are thinking about you, but most people will never say anything to you about the case, and hiding only makes you look guilty."

He was right, but it was hard. Having everyone know

your dirty sexual secrets is rough, and I assumed most people felt disdain for me. Seeing anyone I knew was very embarrassing. People were nice to me and I never had any confrontations, but I honestly wanted to disappear and change my name. I wished I could be someone else and I felt so bad for bringing embarrassment to my family and the Jetton name.

# Chapter 15
# Reaping and Sowing

*"Be not deceived, God is not mocked, for whatever a man soweth, that shall he also reap." – Galatians 6:7*

My bitterness and fighting had made me many political enemies across the state. Those enemies did everything they could to make sure the assault charges ended my political career. Over the last few years, I have had many supporters tell me I was set up by my political opponents. Let me set the record straight: I was not set up by anybody. I arranged to meet this lady on my own, and she was not part of any plan to get me. It is solely my fault and my responsibility.

But once my political opponents learned about the accusation, they took the information and did everything they could to make sure there was an investigation resulting in criminal charges. They used their political power to see me hang...however, I walked to the scaffold, gave them the rope, tied the knot, and put it around my own neck. Had I been in their shoes, I'm sure I would have done the same thing to them.

I remember talking to my good friend, Shannon Cooper, right after my arrest. In an effort to cheer me up he said, "Well Rod, at least things can only get better. You're at rock bottom now, and the only way out is up." While it did seem like my life had hit rock bottom, things were about to get a lot worse.

Two weeks after my arrest I was contacted by a lady I had dated that fall and was given some very sobering news. She told me she was pregnant and that I was going to be a daddy. Wow, that was a big news flash. My son was sixteen at the time and there I was at 42, about to be a new father.

To complicate the situation even more, she was still married. She was separated and in the process of getting a divorce when we started dating. Missouri law prohibits anyone who is pregnant from getting a divorce. It requires that the parties wait until the child is born to do a DNA test to determine who the father is for child support reasons.

This woman came from a good Catholic family, and as you can imagine they were furious with both of us. The only thing they knew about me was what they saw on TV, which was not good. Her divorce, pregnancy and relationship with me were an embarrassment for them, and the whole complicated mess was like something in a soap opera.

For me, it meant another serious talk with my family. I will never forget telling my parents. When my mother heard the news, she gasped like someone had punched her in the gut. I could see the deep disillusionment in her eyes, but there was nothing I could do. What made it even worse for me was the realization that I was causing the woman who had done nothing but love and pray for me my whole life pain.

Once again my children were very kind and supportive. There are just no words to adequately describe how difficult it was to tell my two daughters and teenage son even more details about my whoring around. They were going to have a new sister or brother from someone they really didn't even know, who was still married to another man.

That was one very rough Christmas. I was so thankful for God's forgiveness and so appreciative of my family and friends, but everything else was a total and complete mess. I didn't know what to do about my girlfriend and the arriving baby. She didn't have any place to live so I rented her an apartment to live in and took care of her medical bills. I asked her to marry me, and she said yes, so I made plans to marry her once the baby was born. She was a very nice lady, and I felt responsible to her and the child, but I was adamant about us living apart and not having sex until we were married. By then, I was scared to death of breaking any more of God's commandments.

Right after Christmas, I received more bad news. An old friend called to advise me of a federal grand jury investigation surrounding my handling of a bill regulating Missouri strip clubs during the 2005 legislative session. Over the years, many of my opponents had accused me of misconduct concerning this bill, but nothing had ever come of it. That fall, a rumor about a new investigation had resurfaced, and a friend called to inform me that the FBI was moving forward with it.

I called my attorney who was helping me with the assault case, but he said he was not qualified to handle a federal case. He agreed to call the investigators and check on the situation. Later that week, he confirmed they were investigating the issue and two weeks after that I received a letter in the mail notifying me that I was the target of a federal grand jury investigation. The letter referenced several legal definitions of crimes they were looking into, but it all boiled down to bribery. The letter stated these charges could result in 20-25 years of prison time.

The accusation was that I took a $35,000 donation and promised to kill a bill regulating strip clubs in Missouri. I had been against the bill because it included a tax on strip clubs that I didn't agree with, and the language regulating private businesses seemed unconstitutional to me. I had never been to a strip club and wasn't trying to support them, but my disagreement with the language and my animosity toward Sen. Matt Bartle, the bill's sponsor, were the reasons for my opposition.

Sen. Bartle was a hardcore Christian conservative, and we started out as a very good friends when I sat by him on the House floor during my first two years in Jefferson City. In 2004 when I had problems at home,

Matt was one of the first people I asked to pray for me. Unfortunately, I let a legitimate disagreement on legal reform, along with my judgmental attitude, ruin our friendship.

One of the biggest issues most conservatives were trying to pass in 2004 and 2005 was legal reform. I helped lead the charge in the House, but Matt opposed our efforts in the Senate. He was the chairman of the Senate Judiciary Committee, and we had to make compromises with him to pass a bill. He was a trial attorney, and I decided that he only opposed us because of the money he made suing people. In hindsight, it was a mistake to judge his motives.

Matt Bartle quickly became a rising star in the Republican Party. He gained statewide recognition for opposing stem cell research and was developing a growing following across Missouri. I felt he was only taking some of these conservative positions to further his career and run for attorney general.

Matt also became friends with a few of my enemies from Kansas City, and in my world a friend of my enemy was a new enemy to me. As Speaker, I had power over all bills in the House, and I decided Sen. Bartle would not pass any legislation through the House while I was Speaker. As a Baptist preacher's son and conservative Republican, I should have sat down with Sen. Bartle and worked out these differences, but I didn't want to negotiate with my "enemy." It is sad to look back and see how my pride caused me to lose a friend and be so judgmental.

I didn't support the state relying on a tax revenue from strip clubs, but I also didn't like the good press his bill regulating and taxing strip clubs was getting. I didn't want to see him run for higher office, so I asked my chairman to slow the bill down and take out all the taxes and other extreme regulations.

In the meantime, the strip club owners were in Jefferson City trying to give donations to everyone they could. They thought Bartle's bill would put them out of business, and they needed friends. I told their lobbyist to keep their money. I told them I didn't like Matt Bartle and would kill any of his bills I could. Unfortunately, without me knowing it, the strip club owners made a $35,000 contribution to a political committee that was registered to one of the members of my staff.

At the end of the 2005 session I ended up stripping the taxes and some of the extreme regulations out of Matt's bill and putting that language on a bill I sponsored strengthening punishments for repeat DWI offenders. At the time, I was proud of myself for killing his bill and passing his idea on a bill of my own. Matt was not happy, and I felt satisfied that I had shown him who was boss.

After the campaign reports came out in 2006, Tim Hoover with the *Kansas City Star* wrote a story about the $35,000 contribution, and my opponents started saying I had taken the money to kill the bill. It did look bad, but I had no idea they had even given any money to the campaign. I was furious with my staff, and I had to apologize to the whole caucus. The only thing that saved my credibility with the majority of my caucus was the fact that I had passed the watered down language on my own bill. Now, almost five years later, at the worst possible time for me, the federal government was opening the case back up.

In just over four weeks, I was arrested for assault, found out I was going to be a daddy, and then learned I was facing a possibility of over twenty years in prison. It was very, very discouraging, and I must admit I totally lost hope that January. There was no one to blame but myself. I was reaping what I had sown. My immoral lifestyle led to the assault charge and pregnancy, while my prideful and judgmental attitude against my political enemies led to the federal investigation.

When going through troubles, Christians always say, "Don't worry, God won't put on you any more than you can bear." When I was hopeless, had lost everything, and the whole world seemed to be against me, hearing those words from someone who had no idea how bad my troubles were made me want to slap the person who said it. That advice is taken from 1 Corinthians 10:13 which reads, "There hath no temptation taken you but such is common to man: but God is faithful, who will not suffer you to be tempted above that ye are able; but will with the temptation also make a way to escape, that ye may be able to bear it." In my opinion, this verse isn't talking about handling troubles. I think it is God's promise that He will not allow a person to be tempted beyond what they can resist, that He will provide an escape to keep them from sinning. But if they ignore the escape and give in to temptations, troubles will follow, and troubles will continue to get worse until the sinner gives up, repents and asks God for help.

My troubles had finally forced me to ask God for help. I had nowhere else to turn. I couldn't do anything to stop the grand jury investigation, I couldn't stop the assault charges, and my ability to take care of a wife and a new baby was enormously limited. In the past, when I hit an obstacle or setback, I would work harder and overcome the obstacle, but with my new troubles there was nothing I could do. No amount of better planning, shrewder scheming or harder work would fix my problems. I was at the point where there was nothing I could do.

At that point, I begged God for help. I had finally figured out that my way didn't work. I realized that my pursuit of the things I thought were important, such as pleasure, fortune and fame, was a wild goose chase that ended in failure, embarrassment and pain.

# Chapter 16
# Kindness, Encouragement and Hope

*"A friend loveth at all times, and a brother is born for the day of adversity." – Proverbs 17:17*

Many people who don't go to church or who do not believe in God criticize Christians for being judgmental and unforgiving. Too often those criticisms are warranted because Christians can be the first ones to cast stones, but sometimes those criticisms stem from a person's own guilt or judgmental attitude. When I fell away from my faith, I joined in criticizing Christians for their outspoken condemnation of sin, but once God gave me the grace to see the errors of my ways, I regretted not listening to the warnings I had received and wished they would have been more forceful in turning me away from my own destruction.

When my troubles hit the press, I was very embarrassed and the last place I wanted to be was in church. I thought church was for "good" people, and everyone clearly knew I had not been "good." I reckoned nobody would want me in their church after hearing the accusations against me.

Thankfully, I was wrong. The week after the news broke of my arrest I received a call from my preacher, Bro. Bill Ross, of Harmony Congregational Methodist Church in Marble Hill. I was embarrassed and almost didn't take his call. He stressed God's love and forgiveness while inviting me to church. I remember telling him I didn't think I should come to church and that my presence might upset some of the other members. He replied, "Rod, I think our members know enough about God to be accepting of anyone who has made mistakes, and if they aren't they have a problem. I think you will find everyone will be glad to have you there."

Once I got back to Marble Hill, I reluctantly attended. I remember hearing a choir on the radio sing an old gospel song called Coming Home as I was driving to church that first Sunday. Tears welled up in my eyes and I cried listening to these words:

*I've wandered far away from God,*
*Now I'm coming home;*
*The paths of sin too long I've trod,*
*Lord, I'm coming home.*
*Coming home, coming home,*
*Never more to roam;*

*Open wide thine arms of love,*
*Lord, I'm coming home.*
*I've wasted many precious years,*
*Now I'm coming home;*
*I now repent with bitter tears,*
*Lord, I'm coming home.*
*Coming home, coming home,*
*Never more to roam;*
*Open wide thine arms of love,*
*Lord, I'm coming home.*
*I'm tired of sin and straying, Lord*
*Now I'm coming home;*
*I'll trust thy love, believe thy word,*
*Lord I'm coming home.*
*– William Kirkpatrick*

Once I got to church, I dried my eyes, but when I walked in the door and saw everyone I was so nervous and my heart was beating so hard, I thought it would burst. I knew everyone there had seen the news and heard all the details about my one-night stand. I was extremely scared to talk to any ladies because I could only imagine what they were thinking about a guy who had engaged in rough sex.

Then Tammy Peters came over and talked to me. She is a very godly lady and member of the choir. She walked over to where I was sitting, told me she was glad to see me, and gave me a very nice card. I opened the card and her words of encouragement brought tears to my eyes. I never expected anyone as good as her to be so kind to someone like me.

I'm sure it was awkward for everyone, but they still shook my hand and welcomed me home. The men's Sunday school teacher, Don James, who was also my ex-wife's uncle, was very kind to me, and Elijah Allen, the associate pastor, also treated me with true compassion.

I will never forget the kindness the members of Harmony showed me in those dark days. I have often wondered how I would have treated them if the roles were reversed. I used to be so judgmental. I would read something in the paper or see something on TV and jump to one conclusion: Guilty! I had no mercy, no sympathy, and no compassion. I would have considered a guy like me to be a wicked person who deserved all the punishment he got.

In Matthew 7:1-2, Jesus said, "Judge not, that ye be not judged. For with what judgment ye judge, ye shall be judged: and with what measure ye mete, it shall be measured to you again." Wow, was that verse ever true in my life. I had been such a judgmental person, and now even when I didn't deserve it, God was sending people into my life who were showing me a Christ-like compassion and forgiveness.

Later in 2010, I also received a warm welcome from Pastor Sam Kaunley at The Sanctuary of Hope Church in Branson. I started attending there and didn't think anyone knew about my problems or that I had been in politics, but I was wrong. Pastor Sam was a retired Missouri Highway Patrolman who had served on the security details for Governor's Bond and Ashcroft. He kept up with politics and knew more about me than I realized. I regularly attended church, and was friendly to those around me, but I tried not to draw attention to myself or get too close to anyone, because I wondered what they would think if they knew about my problems.

One Sunday I was walking out after the service when Pastor Sam grabbed me and asked if I had time for lunch that week. We met up at Cracker Barrel where he told me more about his background and said, "Rod, I know all about your case and while you were wrong to be doing what you were doing, I know it's not what it appears." He went on to tell me he had noticed me shuffling into church with my head down, and he said, "You need to hold your head up and realize that God has forgiven you. I could tell you stories about the mistakes almost everyone in that church has made." He finished by explaining that he started The Sanctuary of Hope to minister to those who needed hope as well as God's forgiveness and direction in their life.

I appreciated his thoughtfulness and it did make me feel more comfortable. As time went on, more church people learned about my past, but just as Pastor Sam said, they loved me anyway. It's amazing that when I needed hope I found a church named The Sanctuary of Hope. A church full of faith and forgiveness. A church with Godley men like Bro. Shockley, Pastor Berl Best, Dr. Mike Brown, Dr. Marvin Gorman, Pastor Brad Lombardi and many others who helped me learn more about God's kingdom and His will for my life.

There were others who stepped in and provided encouragement, advice and friendship just when I needed it most. Scott and Harriet Muschany were a gift from God during the darkest days after my fall, and Pastor Ed Klieman's council and advice were a bright light in helping me find my way back to the Lord.

John Bardgett will never know how much he lifted my spirits during those dark days. The day after my grand jury appearance, John called me at 10:30 p.m. and said he heard I didn't have enough money to get a lawyer. He sounded agitated as he almost shouted into the phone, "Mr. Speaker you are one of the most honest Speakers I have ever had the privilege of working with and never in any of my interactions with you did I ever feel like money or donations were a part of the equation. The Lord has been really good to me, and if you need some money to get a good attorney, just let me know."

I laid there in my bed dumbfounded. After reading all the bad things about me in the press and going for days with my phone never ringing, it was nice to hear somebody who had worked with me as Speaker say I was a good guy. He continued by saying, "This whole case is a waste, and I know the kind of people that are out to get you. I don't have a dog in this fight, and I was not involved in that issue so I don't care what they say, if you need any help just let me know."

I was almost in shock, and I muttered back "Thank you so much John. I really appreciate the help and don't know that I'll need it, but your call means a lot."

"No, you don't understand," he emphatically added. "We want you to get a good attorney. Whatever you need just let me know."

"Okay, I'll sure do that. Thanks so much."

As I hung up the phone, I laid there in bed and wondered why a powerful lobbyist who I could do nothing for was willing to risk helping me after all the trouble I was in. In politics once you're out of office and powerless, the friendships, calls and cards stop. They say lobbyists only care about you when you can do something for them, but John Bardgett proved that wrong, because I couldn't do anything for him and yet, he was still willing to stick his neck out for me.

Despite all the bad press, David and Bev Peters were very kind to offer me a place to get away from the world at their secluded home in the woods of Bollinger County. I was out of work, in debt, and living in their basement, which was fully finished with a master suite that was very nice. The press reports were so bad that when they went to work and the babysitter came over, I had to leave because the babysitter's family was concerned for her to be alone there after what they saw about me on TV.

Getting a job with criminal charges pending also proved to be difficult. I applied to drive a garbage truck but never heard back from anyone. I then applied to sell Sears appliances and was extremely excited to be called in for an interview. I met with the manager and had a wonderful interview. Before she told me I had the job I disclosed some details of my assault case. I said, "I want you to know I've been charged with assaulting a woman, but my case hasn't gone to court yet. The accusations against me are not all true, but I made a serious mistake, and put myself in a very bad position."

She replied, "Well thanks for telling me, but I believe a person is innocent until proven guilty."

"I'm glad to hear that, but my case has been on the news, and I just didn't want you to be surprised about it if you found out later."

"I haven't heard anything about it, but as long as you have not been convicted there shouldn't be a problem. I'll call you in two days with a time for you to come in and get your ID made and go through orientation."

That was the first positive news I had received in weeks, and I was walking on cloud nine when I left that interview. I went home and told my kids and parents that I would soon be selling appliances and went online to study the different features of all of the models Sears sold. Two days later she called me and said that unfortunately she couldn't hire me after all. She was such a nice lady, and she apologized saying that with the serious nature of the charge they needed to wait until the issue was cleared up to bring me on. I told her I appreciated the call and understood.

I did understand, but it was still a punch to the gut. All I could do was sing Merle Haggard's song Branded Man and wonder if I would ever get a job again. During those times of disappointment, God always sent someone to encourage me. Right after I lost the Sears job, two people called me who I never would have expected to hear from. The first was Clyde Lear, a very successful businessman who founded Learfield Communications. Each year he organizes the state Governor's Student Leadership Forum for college students across Missouri. I attended the first one as a student in 1988, and he had me speak to the students several times when I was Speaker of the House.

Clyde is a wonderful Christian man who loves the Lord, and while I worked with him on the forum I didn't know him that well, so when he called me I was totally surprised. I answered and he said, "Rod, this is Clyde Lear. I've been following your case and thinking about you, and I just want you to know that you're a good guy and I love you, Brother." I really didn't know what to say.

Here was a very important man in Missouri who I didn't even know that well, taking his time to encourage me after all the terrible mistakes I had made. I mumbled a thank you and apologized for letting him down, but all Clyde said was, "Brother, we all make mistakes. You will get through this, and I just want you to know I love you. If there is anything I can do for you let me know."

A few days later, evangelist Delton Dees called me out of the blue. When I was a young teenager, he came to our church on many occasions. Dad had been good friends with him in the late Seventies and early Eighties, but I had not talked to him in years. I answered his call and he said, "Man, Rod, don't let this get you down. God is a God of second chances." He went on to talk about David and Bathsheba and how God forgave David. He told me to keep praying and stay positive. I was so surprised that an evangelist would care to call me and encourage me.

I'm sure those calls don't seem too significant to anyone else, but I cannot explain how they lifted my spirits at those moments. Their words of love and encouragement gave me hope, and when life gets hard, nothing goes right, and dark clouds are overhead ...hope is a wonderful thing.

# Chapter 17
# Answered Prayers

*"Prayer is of transcendent importance. Prayer is the mightiest agent to advance God's work. Praying hearts and hands only can do God's work. Prayer succeeds when all else fails." – E.M. Bounds*

When Shannon Cooper said I hit rock bottom in December, he may have been a few months early, but by February 2010 I was definitely at rock bottom, and at about that time things started heading up. I will never understand why God was willing to save me from my problems. I was not helping His cause. I did the opposite of what He wanted, and actually was fighting against Him. Had I been God, I would have taken me out of this world. But thankfully, I'm not God. Thankfully, His love is stronger and deeper than anything I can understand.

My testimony had been a very sad one up to this point, but here is where it gets exciting. When I was at the lowest and had lost everything except for my health and my family, when I was facing criminal charges and prison with nowhere else to turn except to

God, He helped me.

God's love for me brought a peace to my life that was indescribable. Even with all of my looming troubles, I had joy, contentment, and a love for others I had never known in all my years leading up to those difficult times.

In desperation, I cried out to God for mercy and just as He promised in the Bible, my prayer was answered. In Matthew 7:7 Jesus said, "Ask, and it shall be given you; seek, and ye shall find; knock, and it shall be opened unto you: For every one that asketh receiveth; and he that seeketh findeth; and to him that knocketh it shall be opened."

I didn't realize it in February, but God was getting ready to show me how very real He was. God showed me how He cared about my needs, and would answer my prayers. He started helping me by forgiving me of my sins when I repented. Then He gave my family the grace they needed to forgive me, and finally, in the worst days when I was feeling the lowest, He sent friends to encourage me just when I needed it most.

**Dad and Mom's Answered Prayer**

The first prayer that was answered was not even my own, but this prayer saved my life. Months before I was arrested, when my life was spiraling out of control, my mom and dad started praying for me. I kept my problems hidden from them, but dad and mom knew my life was messed up, and after my divorce was announced they started praying for God to do whatever it took to get me back on the right path.

I didn't know they were praying this prayer until after my arrest. When things settled down, dad told me what he had asked God to do. Dad was a big fan of a very successful preacher in Florida named Peter Lord. In the Eighties, Peter Lord had shared with dad about his son's struggles with drugs and that no matter what he tried to do, his son continued to run away from God. Peter told dad that he finally asked God to do whatever it took to straighten his son out. A week later his son was arrested and thrown in jail, causing Peter and his church a lot of embarrassment. Eventually, his son got his act together and is now a preacher himself.

Dad said that he also asked God to do whatever it took to get me straightened out. He told me he didn't know it would be me getting arrested, but that he had asked the Lord to do whatever was necessary to get my attention. Mom said that she couldn't pray that prayer because she didn't want to see me get hurt, but that she asked God to help me get my life back on the right track.

In 2009, while my marriage was busting up and my life was spiraling out of control, mom sent me very inspiring cards with Bible verses written on them. It was all very positive and each one was a message filled with love, reminding me about the life I needed to be living. She never nagged or said anything to me, but she didn't have to. I knew mom was telling me to straighten up.

With two Godly parents praying for me I really never had a chance. I thank God they loved me enough to pray that kind of prayer for me. Thankfully, their prayers were answered and assault charges were filed against me. Their prayers and God's answer were the only things that stopped my destruction. Without the assault charge, who knows if I would have ever come to my senses?

**Providing Money**

When I shut down the consulting company in December, I had a $31,000 debt, plus $20,000 in vendor invoices and would soon owe several thousand dollars more in year-end employee bonuses. Many of the clients I worked for owed me money, but I had no way of knowing if they would pay. After all, my problems had caused them political trouble, and they were very disappointed in my actions.

In addition, my divorce decree stipulated that I would pay my wife child support and alimony as well as any taxes owed from 2008 and 2009. Paying all these debts had not been a problem when I was working with a steady income, but with no job and no prospects for one, I had no idea how I would do it.

I took all the money I had and paid the vendors, as well as the employee salaries and bonuses. This left me with a sizable company debt and no money in the bank going into January. Once I went back to church, I received my end of year donations report and realized I had not paid tithes for 2009, which were several thousand dollars. Thankfully, some of my past clients paid me what they owed me, but I wondered if I should use it for my tithes or save it for debts, taxes, child support, legal fees, a new baby, and other unknown expenses. After all, I didn't have a job and had no idea when I would get any more money.

As I said before, by this time I was afraid to do anything wrong and wanted badly to do exactly what God commanded. I also wanted to have the faith that God would take care of me. From the day I got on my knees, repented of my sins, and asked God for help, He answered my prayers. God's love and support caused my faith to grow stronger, but it made no logical sense to give all the money I had to the church when I had been asking God to give it to me in the first place. The smart thing to do was to save it for the major bills I knew were coming. Instead of relying on my own logic, I decided to pray, read my Bible, and asked God for direction. There are three Bible verses I came across that gave me the faith I needed to pay my tithes.

The first was in Malachi 3:7-11, and it seemed to be speaking exactly to my situation. Just like the Israelites, I had ignored God's ordinances, not paid my tithes and gotten into trouble. I wanted to return to God and receive His blessings and that's what Malachi promised. Here are the verses, "Even from the days of your fathers ye are gone away from mine ordinances, and have not kept them. Return unto me, and I will return unto you, saith the LORD of hosts. But ye said, Wherein shall we return? Will a man rob God? Yet ye have robbed me. But ye say, Wherein have we robbed thee? In tithes and offerings. Ye are cursed with a curse: for ye have robbed me, even this whole nation. Bring ye all the tithes into the storehouse, that there may be meat in mine house, and prove me now herewith, saith the LORD of hosts, if I will not open you the windows of heaven, and pour you out a blessing, that there shall not be room enough to receive it. And I will rebuke the devourer for your sakes, and he shall not destroy the fruits of your ground; neither shall your vine cast her fruit before the time in the field, saith the LORD of hosts."

Then in Proverbs it says, "Honour the LORD with thy substance, and with the first fruits of all thine increase: So shall thy barns be filled with plenty, and thy presses shall burst out with new wine." Finally in Luke 6:38 Jesus said, "Give, and it shall be given unto you; good measure, pressed down, and shaken together, and running over, shall men give into your bosom. For with the same measure that ye mete withal it shall be measured to you again."

I thought about those verses and what they meant, and I decided that this was one of the first tests God was putting before me now that I was trying to follow His commands. I never expected to get that money, but I was trusting God for everything else so I did what it says in Malachi, paid my tithes, and entrusted it to God.

Wow was that ever a good decision! Over the next few months God miraculously helped me with my money problems. Cassie was extremely kind to me during this time. She told me she understood my situation and not to worry about sending her any money until I could get back on my feet. Think about how nice that was. I was her ex-husband and my troubles had caused her and the kids a lot of grief, yet she was still willing to be kind to me. I will always remember her thoughtfulness when I needed it most.

In March, I had a job and by April all but two of my clients had paid their bills, and I seriously doubted I would collect on them. I remember saying a special prayer about those collections and within a week the one who owed the most had paid. Then I received a $4,300 check out of the blue from a company I had not even done business with. I quickly cashed the check and then started feeling guilty so I called them and talked to the accounting department about the payment. They promised to look it up but said, "If you received a check it must be correct." I never heard from them again and waited two more months before calling them back and checking again.

As the summer arrived, I paid all the 2008 and 2009 taxes plus I paid Cassie the child support I owed her. Legal fees and doctor bills for my girlfriend were not cheap, but despite all of these challenges I didn't run out of money. I wasn't rich and I cleaned out all my savings accounts, but at least I didn't go bankrupt. Heading into June, things looked a lot better than they had in February.

## Sending Me a Job

Allow me to back up a little bit. After the end of Febuary, I was thinking I may never find a job. Then, without even sending him a résumé, Stan Schultz called me and asked if I would have time to meet with him about working for his engineering company. Time was one thing I had plenty of, so I met with him and his partner, Bob Summers. They explained that their company was growing, but they needed help developing business in their New Orleans and Branson offices.

Stan said, "Rod, I have looked into your case, and know this will all be behind you shortly. If you would be willing to help our company for a year or two, I think we could take our operation to the next level." He went on to explain they would want me to immediately go to Louisiana and track down work for their New Orleans office.

Having someone actually wanting me to join their team was really nice and going to New Orleans where me and my troubles were unknown sounded appealing. I didn't know exactly what they needed, but I had always been involved in some sort of sales and told them I would take the job.

I will always be grateful to Stan and Bob for bringing me on at that time in my life. I'm convinced that God opened that door for me, and I was excited about the opportunity. They were very trusting owners because I started with Schultz and Summers Engineering (SSE) on March 8, and on March 10 I had to be in Kansas City to testify to the grand jury. I remember calling Stan and telling him I was headed to Kansas City and hoped I would be back, but there was a chance they would let me testify and then indict me. I told him I had no money for bail and that I would just stay in jail and have a public defender represent me. He wished me well and off to Kansas City I went.

## Peace for the Grand Jury

I mentioned earlier that my lawyer had no experience with a federal criminal case and couldn't represent me in federal proceedings, but after telling him the facts he agreed to contact the investigators and let them know that I would be happy to sit down and answer any questions about the case. I thought that once they heard the truth, they would see there was no reason for a grand jury. Unfortunately, it seemed like they didn't want to talk to me; they wanted to indict me.

My attorney also strongly recommended that I not testify to the grand jury. He offered to check with some lawyers who did that kind of work and found out they wouldn't even agree to talk to me without a $40,000 retainer. I couldn't afford that, so off I went to Kansas City against the recommendation of my attorney and without a lawyer advising me.

Describing what it was like to testify to a grand jury after everyone told me that they wanted to indict me is almost impossible. It was a highly stressful and daunting event. Without the Lord's grace, I never could have handled the pressure. I spent the night with my good friend Jim Dusek from Excelsior Springs, Missouri, and drove down to the federal courthouse in Kansas City the next morning.

As I walked to the door, I noticed the press were waiting for me, and before I could get inside I was surrounded by reporters and TV cameras. I told them I couldn't comment and fought my way inside as fast as I could. I went through the metal detectors and took the elevator to the jury room. Someone ushered me into a waiting room and informed me it would be a few minutes before the jury was ready for me.

As I sat there by myself, I prayed hard. I asked God to give me a clear mind to answer their questions correctly and that the jury members and investigators would see the truth. I asked God to help me trust in Him and to keep me calm. I held out my hand to see if I could hold it steady, and surprisingly it was not shaking. The Lord gave me peace as I walked through the door, but I can tell you that sitting there answering questions was one of the most stressful things I have ever done.

I sat in front of 25 average citizens who were all looking at me, while two lawyers asked me all kinds of questions and details about the legislation. The process lasted over an hour, and after it was over they asked me not to talk with anyone about what I was asked. Since I don't want to get in any more trouble, I won't go into the details. Just know that when I came out of that room, I had no idea what would happen to me. They never said, "Thanks for coming," "This clears things up," or "Please stay in the waiting room because we are going to arrest you." I really had no idea what would happen. I ended up staying at Jim's house another night just in case they indicted me.

I didn't get arrested and the statute of limitations ran out on the charges later that year, so I guess it all went fine. Most of my friends in the legal community couldn't believe I testified without the help of a lawyer and they often tell me how brave I am, but the only thing that got me through that ordeal was God! I told the truth, and I believe God allowed the jury members to see that I was telling the truth. It was not me, but God's grace that carried me through that ordeal.

## Preparing for a Baby

Learning that I was going to have a baby should have been exciting, but learning that I was going to have a baby at the age of 42, when the child's mother was married to someone else and while I was facing criminal assault charges as well as a federal grand jury, took away the excitement.

Let me ask you a question. What does God want you to do when you get a lady pregnant and she is still married to another man? What is the right thing to do? Do you marry her? It may sound like something on a soap opera or a Jerry Springer episode, but it was real life for me, and I wanted to do the right thing. But what was the right thing? There were many reasons to marry her. She was an extremely nice lady, hard-working, a good mother, and very beautiful inside and out. Like me, she was going through a rough time at home and had gotten off track, making big mistakes.

I decided that I should marry my girlfriend after the baby was born when she could get divorced from her husband. It wasn't an easy decision for several reasons. Was it right to bust up her family? Would my children like her? Would my family accept her? What would her family think?

After I asked her to marry me, I rented her an apartment and made sure she found a good doctor. Then we settled in to wait for a baby to be born and made plans to marry. My criminal problems and their outcome also weighed heavily on my mind. I was very adamant about us not living together or having sex, and she agreed with me about that. We were both trying to get our lives back on track.

My family was very kind to her, and her father was nice to me. We spent a lot of time together when I was not working in New Orleans, and things seemed to settle down after I learned the grand jury was not going to indict me. Each morning I started my day by reading my Bible and praying for God to help me through my troubles, and each night I asked God to forgive me of any sin in my life, then I would fall asleep reading the Bible or some other spiritual book.

One of my prayer requests each morning was for me to love my girlfriend and be a good husband. I remember toward the end of April I started having an uneasy feeling about that prayer. I can't describe what I felt, but it just didn't seem right so I changed my morning prayer and asked God if marrying her was what He wanted me to do.

I keep a diary with prayer requests and answered prayers and on May 18, 2010, as I was praying, I believe God gave me an answer about marriage. I had a peace that I was not supposed to marry my girlfriend. She already had a husband and while we had definitely made a mistake, two wrongs don't make a right.

I was in New Orleans that week and decided that I would wait until the baby was born to tell her, because I didn't want her upset while she was pregnant since she had no place to live and nobody to help her. My plan was to tell her after the baby was born and we could arrange child support and visitation. I hoped that maybe she could save her family.

The next morning as I was praying about her and the baby I felt God leading me to tell her that weekend. If you have never had an experience like this you are probably thinking I am crazy. Before my troubles if you had told me a story like this, I wouldn't have made fun of you, but I would have been thinking that you were a little off.

When I got back to Missouri and explained that we could not get married, my girlfriend was upset, just as I thought she would be. I reassured her that I would still help with all her expenses and that after the birth we could do visitation and child support. I explained my prayers and that I felt God was telling me that she still had a family and that our marriage would not be right.

It was a rough time for her. She was pregnant, emotional, her family was upset, and her husband wanted nothing to do with her. After she calmed down,

I left. Over the next week, I still called and texted her to make sure she was okay, but I didn't see her much.

Amazingly, she had dinner with her husband the first week of June. Then she told me they had talked and he wanted to try and work things out. By the beginning of July, she had moved some of her things back into their house and by the end of July moved out of the apartment and fully into her house.

In July she told me there was a slight chance it could be her husband's baby, because they had slept together once that November, which made me think that God might have known something when He led me to break off the marriage. We all waited for the baby to be born so we could find out if I was the father.

While the news of a baby seemed like more trouble, it was a blessing in disguise for me. In January and February, when I had no hope, the thought of having a baby gave me hope. I knew I deserved all my troubles, but I could not understand why God would let a guy in my position have a baby. Why would somebody who couldn't get a job and might be spending twenty years in prison be given a baby? I didn't think God would do that to a baby and that thought gave me hope. I thought God must still have something for me to do. My troubles made me feel as if I were down at the bottom of a deep pit with no way to climb out or even get a toehold to try. Dark clouds had gathered over the only part of the sky I could see from my hole and then God dropped a rope down into my pit. I wasn't out of my pit and that rope didn't even mean I could climb out, but it gave me hope when it seemed like my life was over ... and hope, at that time in my life was a wonderful thing.

The baby was born in September, and the DNA test determined that her husband was the father. God had worked everything out. Had we not broken up in May when I felt God leading me, she and her husband would have not had time to work things out and get back together by the time the baby was born. She would have been with me and had his baby, which would have been a disaster.

Do you really think all those events were just a coincidence? Do you think the Lord impressing me during my prayer time that we shouldn't get married was just a hunch, or that her husband being willing to take her back was just luck? That the thought of being a father to a new baby accidently gave me hope when I needed it most? I never dreamed her husband would take her back in May, and I sure didn't know it wouldn't be my baby. Now, do you see why I have more peace in my life? I have more faith in God, and faith in God helps me accept that even when life doesn't go as I planned, things will work out for the best in the end. The hardest part is making sure my plan is God's plan.

## Healing My Back

In the summer of 2010, I mostly traveled between New Orleans and Branson. Wherever I was, I tried to find a church to attend on Wednesday nights, and that's the summer I started attending the Sanctuary of Hope Church I wrote about earlier. I really enjoyed

Pastor Sam Kaunley's preaching.

The Sanctuary is called a spirit-filled church because they believe in healing people by praying for them. When I started attending, I didn't know they were a spirit-filled church. In fact, I had no idea what a "spirit-filled church" was. I just thought they were friendly, and I liked the preaching. Furthermore, I was raised as a Baptist and while I believed that Jesus healed people in the Bible, I had never seen anyone healed and I thought that kind of thing only happened in biblical times or in foreign countries.

One Wednesday night in October, I headed to Branson and ended up getting to church late. I snuck in and sat toward the back. That night they had a guest preacher I didn't know. One of the elders, Bro. Charles Shockley, was preaching and gave a very interesting sermon that I enjoyed. At the end, he closed and said, "I've been praying for two days for a lady who was in the service tonight." He informed us that we would have a healing service as he called her up to pray for God to heal her painful back.

He also called up another lady who had back problems, as he explained God's healing power and told a story about how his wife had been healed of her back problems through prayer. The first lady had a brace on and couldn't even stand up straight. She was bent over almost at a 90 degree angle as she slowly shuffled up to the front. Bro. Shockley then placed his hand on her head and said a short prayer. It was not a loud or long prayer, and when he was finished she stood up, touched her toes and said she felt much better.

He did the same thing for the other lady and she also said she was better. He then said he had not planned on this but felt the Lord leading him to ask if anyone else needed their back healed.

I watched all this with skepticism and was wondering if it was real, while telling God I was sorry for being so skeptical. I told myself it must be real because who would put on a show for forty people in a small church on a Wednesday night? I could tell the first lady had been in pain as she hobbled to the front, and I saw her stand up straight and touch her toes after he prayed for her. I also didn't think she or Bro. Shockley had any reason to try and deceive anyone, but this was hard to believe.

When he asked if anyone else was having back problems I immediately thought about how bad my back had been hurting. For the last year I had been dealing with a bad sciatic nerve problem. I had visited my chiropractor and physical therapist for numerous treatments and they had helped, but it was still bothering me. It caused my hip to hurt badly and made it hard to run without pain. I had even been praying for the last eight months for it to get better, but nothing improved.

My first thought was I should let the older people who really needed help, go up for prayer. Then I asked myself why not go up? Why not give this a try? I had been asking for God to help my back get better and maybe this was Him answering my prayers. As I stepped out into the aisle, I prayed the same prayer the father who brought his son to be healed by Jesus prayed in Mark 9:24 when he said with tears in his eyes, "Lord, I believe; help thou mine unbelief."

There were six of us who walked up to the front of the church for prayer. Bro. Shockley sat us all down on the front row and started praying for each person's problem. I was fifth in line. When he got to me he asked, "Son, what do you need healing for?" I said, "I have been praying for my lower back, but it hasn't gotten better."

He asked me to sit then he kneeled, looked at my legs, and said one was shorter than the other. I added, "My chiropractor said the same thing." He told me that many back problems were because one leg was shorter than the other. Bro. Shockley said he was going to pray to the chiropractor on high and God would heal me if I believed.

I kept praying for the Lord to help my unbelief. I expected him to lay his hands on my head or shout something out loud, but Bro. Shockley only put his hands under my heels. He said a very quiet and matter-of-fact prayer asking God to heal my back. There was really nothing special about it, but as he prayed I felt a twitch or spasm of electricity, kind of like a shock, shoot down my right leg, which was the longer one. I didn't say anything to him about this, but right after that happened he said, "One leg is getting shorter to match the other one." He added, "Don't worry, they will even out in just a bit."

Soon he told me they were both the same length and asked me to stand up. I stood up and walked around feeling better, but I was still skeptical. I told him, "It feels good, but until I go for a run I won't know for sure if it's better."

He then went to the last person who was a lady with one leg longer than the other. He asked me to stand over his shoulder and watch as he prayed. I could clearly see that one of her legs was almost a half inch longer than the other one. As he prayed, I watched her shorter leg get longer until it was even with her other one. Bro. Shockley held his hands under her feet as he prayed and I double checked to see if he was pulling her feet, but he didn't pull them at all. I had also not felt any pulling on my legs. Once he finished praying, her legs were even so he asked her to stand up and walk around just like me.

Bro. Shockley did all this in a very calm, matter-of-fact way. There was no shouting, shoving with people falling down or anything crazy like I had expected from watching TV. He did have a very small vile of anointing oil, but he never used it on me. It was as if he had no doubt about people being healed and this was just a normal thing for him to do. For me, it was far from normal. I could not deny what I had seen, and what I had seen and experienced was exciting! That service increased my faith, and I couldn't help but wonder why God would do something like that for a sinner like me. Once again, He answered my prayers and showed His unconditional love for me.

After the service I went up to introduce myself and thank Bro. Shockley, but he said, "Don't thank me, thank God, He healed you." I was very glad I ended up in that service that night. The next day I went out for a hard seven-mile run and had no pain. I kept running and didn't have pain. Even after a car wreck later that month my back pain was gone! As you can imagine, I wanted to attend that church and get to know Bro. Shockley better after that. Later, he told me why he had me come and watch the other lady's legs after I was healed. He said seeing her legs even out would help me believe that all things are possible.

I know this story sounds crazy and unbelievable. Before this happened, I would have thought that, too. Yet after all the things God had done for me since my repentance, I had just enough faith and curiosity to go up and give it a try. I felt the jolt in my leg, I watched his hands on the other lady's feet. I have no reason to lie about it, and I am sure I wasn't deceived. It is another amazing display of God's grace and love in my life.

## Plea Bargain on the Assault Charge

One thing I have learned about our court system is that justice moves slowly. As 2010 came to a close, my case had still not gone to court. A dark cloud hung over my head every morning when I woke up, but having troubles and needing God to help me with something that was out of my control was teaching me a good lesson in faith and taking one day at a time.

I entered a plea of innocent from the start and felt that everything we had done that night was consensual, but let me be clear, there was nothing right or okay with what I did that night. It was totally wrong to be meeting with a woman I barely knew to have illicit sex. It was even more wrong to be discussing rough sex and safe words. This was just another part of what can happen when divorced adults who are hurting and depressed do very stupid things to deal with their pain.

I have asked myself hundreds of times since my arrest how I fell down into the immoral life I was living. How could someone who had been teaching a young boys' Sunday school class only eight years before do some of the terrible and immoral things I did when I was living a life of sin? Just a few years before, I was a loving husband and a good father, but somehow I threw that away and embraced a life of wickedness that left me feeling empty and alone.

The prosecutor charged me with a class C felony assault charge that allows up to seven years of jail time. During the preliminary hearing, they offered me a plea deal for a felony conviction with a possible six month prison sentence and probation for two years. I turned that down, went through with the preliminary hearing, and did my best to dodge all the press and cameras as I left the courthouse.

Nothing much happened for several months, and then the lady who filed the charges had to come in for her deposition. This is when my lawyer asked her questions about her accusations and her police statement. Soon after that, I was offered another plea deal for a class C felony conviction that included no jail time and a very short probation. I again turned that down because I felt that once a jury heard the whole story, they would not convict me of a crime. I had no doubt they would think I was a terrible person, but not that I had committed a crime.

As 2011 approached, the case was still dragging on. That winter, I was offered another plea deal for a class A misdemeanor conviction with no jail time and short probation. By that time, I had spent a fortune in legal fees and was determined to take my case to a jury. In April, I received a call from my attorney, Steve Wilson, telling me they had offered a new deal he didn't think I could turn down. He said, "Rod, if you will plead guilty to a class C misdemeanor assault charge (which is the lowest class) they'll give you a Suspended Imposition of Sentencing (SIS). That means you will not be convicted of a crime and will not have a criminal record."

I asked him how in the world I could plead guilty to a crime and not have a conviction on my record. He gave me a very proper and legal explanation, but to me it came down to a way for prosecutors to get guilty pleas from first-time offenders and move on to another case without having a jury trial. I replied, "I don't think I want to say I'm guilty."

"Rod, they are offering you something I have never seen in all my years of legal work, and as your attorney I have to advise you to accept it. They are willing to hold a special hearing just for this case and as soon as you plead guilty and pay court costs, your probation will be over and this case will be closed. The press will not be there and no one will be able to get the records for the case once it's closed."

"Do you think it's a good deal?"

"Yes, I do. Normally an SIS has a year or two for probation, and during that time the case is open and the press can request all the records. But in this case, once you pay court costs your probation is over. We're probably talking about twenty minutes. I think this is the best way to get this case behind you."

"Do you think I can win with a jury?"

"I think we have a very strong case, but anytime you're at the mercy of a jury it can go either way. I think we have a better chance of winning it, but I can't guarantee a win, and a jury trial will cost you a lot more money. If you take this deal now, the case is over and you can move on with your life."

As I hung up, his words about having the case behind me, saving money and moving on with my life sounded really nice. But I did not want to plead guilty. I wondered if I was supposed to take this deal or if my pride was the only thing telling me not to. I had a good friend who, like me, was in the wrong place at the wrong time, doing something he never should have done. He was accused of some very bad crimes that he did not commit and, like me, plead not guilty. He was offered several plea bargains along the way and turned them all down. He finally went to court and was found innocent. While he was very thankful to be found innocent, in the end he said it really didn't matter. He told me that his true friends didn't care that he was found, because they already believed him. All the others he was worried about never cared or believed that he was innocent. He explained that all the disbelievers thought he was another criminal who had "beat" the system. He thought that if I went to trial and won, most people would say I got off because of my connections not because I wasn't guilty. He seemed to think spending the money to fight it out wasn't worth it.

I talked to my family about it, and they were for getting the case behind me. I also prayed for guidance and asked God to tell me what to do. Bro. Shockley is someone who I spent time with learning more about the Bible. I told him about my troubles and asked him to pray for me. One Sunday morning I told him about the latest plea deal and he told me something that had a big impact on my decision: "Rod, I don't know what this means, but as you were talking a scripture popped into my head that you need to hear." He quoted Matthew 5:25, "Agree with thine adversary quickly, whiles thou art in the way with him; lest at any time the adversary deliver thee to the judge, and the judge deliver thee to the officer, and thou be cast into prison."

I felt like that scripture coming from a man who clearly had a connection with God was the direction I needed. It reinforced all the advice from friends and family. I could see my pride was preventing me from taking a very good deal that would get this case behind me. I called my lawyer and told him to proceed.

I showed up at the New Madrid courthouse on May 26, 2011, for the 9:30 a.m. hearing. I brought enough cash to pay the court costs and restitution specified in the deal. I had to have cash because once I paid the fines, my probation would be over. The only people in the courtroom were the clerks, the prosecutor, the judge, my attorney and the lady I had spent the night with.

I approached the bench, and the judge asked me if I knew what I was doing. I said I did. I was prepared to say I was guilty, but it was harder than I expected. The judge asked me if I was guilty about four different ways so there could be no question that I understood what I was admitting to. The first one was the hardest, and I was glad when that process was over.

As I turned around and walked away from the bench I told the lady I was sorry for any problems I had caused her, and I also apologized to the prosecuting attorney for having to deal with my case. Then I left with my attorney to pay the fine. I was glad the case was closed, and I'm sure she was just as happy as I was to move on with our lives.

I was sorry for my mistake, sorry for dishonoring God, and sorry for doing anything to cause her problems. What we talked about doing was wrong and I regret my actions that night. The consequences were the worst thing to ever happen to me, but in the end her accusations brought my immoral lifestyle to light, and without that happening, who knows where I might have ended up?

## Success in Business

Another way God answered my prayers was by blessing my work at Schultz and Summers Engineering (SSE). When I joined SSE, they were a growing company that had a very good story to tell. They needed help building a marketing program, expanding their business development team and telling their story. I asked God to give me the wisdom to help them organize their sales efforts and expand their business.

We built a customer database, upgraded the website, put together a contact plan, and reformatted the proposal and presentation process. I spent hours writing biographies, stories and press releases highlighting SSE's accomplishments that we could send to the press, include in our newsletter or post on the new company blog and social media channels.

I also went on sales calls, planned events, sent out emails and put together advertising plans that brought in more work for the company. Our sales numbers went up and company revenue doubled, allowing SSE to make the Inc. 500/5000 list in 2010, 2011 and 2012. Stan and Bob were very happy with my work, and I very much enjoyed my co-workers and the things we were accomplishing at SSE. I was even recognized by the *Springfield Business Journal* as the top Marketing Director in Southwest Missouri in 2011.

When I received the award, my daughter, Emily, was there as well as my mom and dad. Finally, after all the embarrassment and trouble I had caused them, they had a reason to be proud of me again. Thankfully, I didn't let my business success go to my head. I knew the only reason things were going so well was because of God's blessings. I spent a lot of time praying about my efforts at SSE. I even had a list of friends I would text asking them to pray for all our big sales calls before we gave our presentation. Those prayers were answered and we were awarded the biggest projects in the company's history during the three years I worked at SSE.

I worked hard, but I also took time to be with my family, and most importantly, I didn't get too busy to pray. I had forgotten how peaceful working in the private sector could be compared to politics. In politics, there is no second place. If you lose your campaign, you are out of a job. That is why campaigns and politics can be so destructive. The winner has the power and makes the rules while the loser is thrown out and has to follow the rules they don't agree with.

In business, you win some contracts and lose others. Maybe you get 30 percent of the business and maybe you get 60 percent, but you're still in business. You can lose customers one month and find new customers the next month. Imagine if we had an election between Pepsi and Coke and the brand that won would be the only brand anyone could drink for the next four years. I bet the ad campaigns would get a bit more desperate, and the Coke or Pepsi drinkers would openly fight with each other, because one of them would be going out of business after that election.

Working in an industry where everyone was a professional—where they competed against each other but were not trying to ruin each other—was very peaceful. It was such a blessing and made me so very thankful to be out of politics. I worked hard and prayed hard, and the Lord blessed me with tremendous business success, wonderful co-workers, and a chance to start rebuilding my life.

## Other Blessings

Having my clients pay their bills, being hired by SSE, and avoiding bankruptcy are things I am very thankful for, but getting through the grand jury testimony and not being convicted of a crime in the assault case, as well as enjoying tremendous business success were incredible answers to my prayers. What God did for a sinner like me is amazing.

But those wonderful gifts were only preparing me for the major blessings God gave me when He provided direction on the issue of marrying my girlfriend and healed my back. These are some of the "big" miracles I believe God did for me after I turned back to Him. But there were many other blessing I received that strengthened my faith.

Even though Eric paid all our vendors when I shut down the consulting company, I found out that there was an additional $1,200 bill that one vendor didn't know about, but later realized was outstanding. I talked with them about it and made arrangements to pay it over a few months. A few weeks after that I received an email from Cherie Snyder, who I had let borrow some office equipment when I shut my operation down.

In her email she asked me if she could go ahead and purchase the equipment. She had prepared a breakdown of what she thought everything was worth. It totaled $1,150, which was almost exactly what the vendor bill was. I emailed her back and said I would be happy to sell it if she would come up to $1,200. She said yes and I then explained why I had asked for the extra $50 bucks. I used that money to pay the vendor.

When I started with SSE, I had no health insurance for me or my kids. I was praying for God to keep us in good health, and thankfully, He answered that prayer. I had to work for 90 days before I qualified for company insurance and on my 91st day of work my son, Will, got sick and had to go to the doctor. Fortunately, he was covered!

During this whole time, going to church took on a whole new meaning for me. In the past, I complained about church a lot. Either the singing was not what I wanted or the preacher went too long, or people bothered me with questions. I spent most of the service checking my phone or thinking about the football games I was going to watch if the preacher would just hurry up and wrap things up. I didn't get much out of church, but I didn't put much into it either.

After I repented, I went to church with a whole new

attitude. I found I really enjoyed services and no matter the singing style or sermon topic, God seemed to speak to my heart. I focused on the words to the music more and sometimes while singing tears would just well up in my eyes. There were numerous times when I was praying for something and the preacher's sermon would be an answer to that prayer, providing me the exact direction on what I was supposed to do.

I went to very formal churches and very laid back churches, but it didn't seem to matter. When they sang about Jesus and the cross, it touched me, and when they opened the Bible I learned things. I made a rule to never look at my phone during a church service and even got a notebook and took notes. It's amazing how much more I got out of church when I went there focused on worshiping God and expecting to learn more about His commandments.

There have been many, many other answered prayers. I don't have space here to tell all of them, but all of these experiences strengthened my faith and brought peace into my life.

Before my troubles, I prayed many times and asked God for help, but when I didn't get an answer I either blamed God for not answering me or chalked it up to my request not being His will. Since I have drawn closer to God and learned more about his promises, I believe my lack of answers had more to do with sin and unforgiveness in my life than God's will or lack of interest. In retrospect I can see that when I was on the right path I received answers to my prayers, and when

I drifted away from the Lord, I didn't get many answers.

# Chapter 18
# Forgiveness

*"But if a wicked man turns away from all the sins he has committed and keeps all my decrees and does what is just and right, he will surely live; he will not die. None of the offenses he has committed will be remembered against him. Because of the righteous things he has done, he will live. Do I take any pleasure in the death of the wicked? Declares the sovereign Lord. Rather am I not pleased when they turn from their ways and live?"* – *Ezekiel 18 21-23NIV*

While pride was my biggest problem, bitterness and unforgiveness were very good friends of my pride and contributed mightily to my downfall. For me, the bitterness snuck in unnoticed and quickly took root, before I realized it was there. As it grew, I became very unforgiving and judgmental. Those attitudes led me to hold grudges, pick fights and be very impatient with those around me. Anyone who hurt me or did anything against me became my enemy, which led to more fights, more bitterness and more unforgiveness.

I never realized how important forgiveness was to Jesus until I started reading the New Testament more closely. He spent considerable time talking about forgiveness in His teachings. He included forgiving others in the Lord's Prayer and then when He finished the Lord's Prayer Jesus added, "For if ye forgive men their trespasses, your heavenly Father will also forgive you: But if ye forgive not men their trespasses, neither will your Father forgive your trespasses."

Over and over again, Jesus gave commands to forgive when He said, "Love your enemies, turn the other cheek, and bless them that curse you, or do unto others as you would have them do to you." I remembered the Bible stories of how Jesus forgave the woman caught in adultery, or the thief on the cross. In the eighteenth chapter of Matthew, Jesus told a parable about the unforgiving servant which ended with these words, "Shouldest not thou also have had compassion on thy fellow servant, even as I had pity on thee? And his lord was wroth, and delivered him to the tormentors, till he should pay all that was due unto him. So likewise shall my heavenly Father do also unto you, if ye from your hearts forgive not everyone his brother their trespasses."

Unforgiveness and bitterness sure tormented me. It was always eating me up on the inside and caused me to lash out at those around me. I let the anger and animosity I held for my enemies spill over on my family and friends. Finally, my arrest broke me and showed me how wicked I had been. Once I realized how God had forgiven me despite my wickedness, it was hard to be mad or judgmental with any of my enemies. It may sound strange, but my attitude quickly changed about people who I had been convinced had done me wrong. As I grew closer to the Lord, I started seeing how my fights were not all my enemies' fault, and how my attitude or actions led to or escalated those conflicts. As I prayed, the Lord put certain people on my mind who I knew I needed to apologize to.

I still had lots of pride, and I sure didn't want to apologize, but I couldn't run from the conviction I felt in church services or during my prayer time. I sent an email to several of my donors and key supporters apologizing for letting them down. I also called Pastor Elmo Parker who I had let down with my actions after he had been very supportive in my first race. First and foremost, I apologized to my ex-wife. I also went and talked to Senator Brad Lager who I had fired as the Budget Chairman in 2005 along with Scott Lipke who I removed as chairman of the crime committee, Representative Dennis Woods who I fought with over the controversial village law legislation, Representative Jim Viebrock who I kicked out of his office, David Barkledge and Jeff Roe who were campaign consultants who I fought with over campaigns, Senator Bartle who I wrongly judged, and Senator David Pearce who had been nothing but a good friend to me, and yet I designed some very nasty fliers against him in 2008.

I also had to deal with my angry feelings for those involved in my assault case. I had to deal with the lady who accused me of assault, the prosecutor and my political opponents who did all they could to encourage the prosecutor to charge me with a crime. I also had to deal with some of the people who I felt had pushed the FBI to reopen the federal case against me.

For Pastor Parker, my donors and past supporters, it wasn't so much a matter of me forgiving them as much as me feeling like I needed to apologize. It was also fairly easy to forgive those involved in my criminal cases, because it didn't take me long to realize had I not had those legal troubles, I may never have gotten my life straightened out. I don't think my enemies were trying to help me, but they did me a huge favor. The devil used pride and my strengths to get me off track, but God used the enemies created by my pride to get me back on track.

The hardest people to forgive were those who I felt had double-crossed me, stabbed me in the back, or used me and my position to advance their interests. My marriage problems left me with bitter feelings toward my wife, and I had been carrying grudges against many state legislative leaders who I had fought with over the years. As I made calls, sent letters and visited with all these people, I found they were extremely gracious in their willingness to overlook my past actions. Surprisingly, many of them hadn't thought much about me or our "fights." Those feelings and grudges I felt had only been hurting me all that time.

Once my eyes were opened to the hypocrite I had been, and I lost my judgmental attitude, I could better see where I had been at fault in many of these situations. I remember saying or doing things that escalated fights and caused more hard feelings. The relief and joy I felt as I let those bitter feelings go made me feel as light as a feather. It is one of the reasons I have so much more joy and happiness in my life now.

There was one person who I had an extremely hard time forgiving. I tried to forgive him, and thought I had many times, but I just couldn't let it go because he had done more to let me down than anyone else. I trusted him, but when temptations came and things didn't go as planned, he failed me. Many times when thinking about all my troubles I wanted to beat him to death, because I knew he should have known better. He had always come through for me in the past, before I was important and powerful, but now, after my troubles it was very, very hard to forgive him. After all, he was the main reason for all of my pain and problems. The guy I am talking about is me.

I found forgiving myself to be tough. I had always been a success, I had always been the leader of the team. In high school track, college track, college student government, the Marine Corps, business, and then in the Missouri House, I had never been the weak link. I had always been the star, always helped everyone else, but now I was the problem. I was the weak link. There was nobody else to blame, and no matter how many times I ran scenarios through my mind about what I could have done differently, it always came back to my mistakes, my weaknesses, or my shortcomings.

God had forgiven me, my family had forgiven me, friends had forgiven me, but I had a hard time forgiving myself. In Matthew 22: 37-39, the lawyer asked Jesus which was the greatest commandment and Jesus said, "Thou shalt love the Lord thy God with all thy heart, and with all thy soul, and with all thy mind. This is the first and great commandment. And the second is like unto it, Thou shalt love thy neighbor as thyself." Once Brother Shockley was talking with me about that Bible verse and stressing forgiveness when he asked me, "Rod, have you forgiven yourself?"

I replied, "I think so?"

"You need to make sure, because you will not be able to love anyone else, if you can't love yourself."

I spent a lot of time praying and thinking about forgiving myself. It took a while, but I finally was able to forgive myself for all my mistakes. The weight of guilt and remorse that was lifted from my shoulders made me feel as if I was almost floating up to heaven. I have learned forgiveness is such an important part of God's kingdom, and I pray I never forget how good it feels to forgive others and myself, or to turn the other cheek and to help those who are opposing me.

# Chapter 19
# Paul Norman

*"Truth sits upon the lips of dying men." – Matthew
Arnold*

L ife has new meaning for me now. I look at things
from a totally different angle. I still have the same
temptations, same tendencies, and same struggles
I had before, but my goals are different. What used to
be important to me is not as important anymore.
Prominence, popularity and prosperity do not hold the
same luster they used to.

Losing everything will change how a person thinks. I
have talked to others who have lost everything or
almost died, but for some reason were given a second
chance. Each of them gives basically the same type of
advice. Enjoy each day, think about eternity, be more
encouraging, take time to thank God, help others,
spend more time with your family, and consider the
troubles of others.

Why did it take a personal tragedy for me to realize
what's important in life? When I was at my lowest,
whenever I heard of others' tragedies I realized my

troubles weren't really that bad. Each day I would hear about a child with cancer, or a family who lost their mother, father or child in a tragic car accident, or a serviceman killed in combat. I was reminded that my self-inflicted troubles were not nearly as rough as what those families were going through. After all, I was still breathing, my family was healthy and God had forgiven me.

One such person who has stayed on my mind was one of my staff members, Paul Norman. Paul was a young kid who joined my staff while he was in college and then came on full time after he graduated. He was an extremely smart kid, but very quiet. Paul was a hard worker and did a great job with whatever I tasked him with. He was a thinker and a very good writer. He didn't talk much, but he had grand ideas about how to help make me the next governor of Missouri. He was very loyal and poured his life into helping me succeed.

Unfortunately, he was diagnosed with leukemia in August 2006 and struggled through numerous hospital stays, bone marrow transplants and drug therapies. Thankfully, the leukemia went into remission the next August, and he was able to get back to politics, which he loved. Then, just when he was hired by Victory Enterprises as a consultant, his cancer came back.

I went to see Paul several times when he was in the hospital. His treatments and the leukemia had him worn down, and I'm sure he was feeling bad, but he always seemed upbeat and never complained about his situation. I don't know why God took Paul Norman from us. He was a much better person than me. I want to include an email Paul sent me a month before he died at the age of 28 on June 16, 2008. His final words to me are a powerful testimony and I would ask that you pay special attention to the last line of his email. In 2008 when I read those lines, they left me feeling awfully guilty about my life, because I knew he was right. Now, I try to live my life in such a way as to follow Paul Norman's advice:

**From:** Paul Norman
[mailto:paulenorman@hotmail.com]
**Sent:** Friday, May 16, 2008 1:43 PM
**To:** Chris Benjamin; Dave Hageman; Eric Brooks; Jason Crowell; Kay Fitzpatrik; Nicole Brown; Rod Jetton; Ross McFerron; Wayne Yocum
**Subject:**

Friends,

I had previously told many of you my initial reluctance to pursue one last treatment because there existed the risk that it could greatly reduce the amount of time I have left. My medical team's final plan was to induce remission with chemo, and then perform radiation and a second bone marrow transplant. The overall likelihood of this working was 30 percent, but I had a 60 percent chance of going into remission to buy time. Upon remission, I would have the stem cell transplant performed with a different donor at Barnes Jewish in

St. Louis, one of the top 5 transplant centers in the world. After hearing the course of action, I felt comfortable in my decision to proceed and felt there was plenty of hope with this treatment.

The day after I was released from the hospital, I was given some bad news. The bone marrow biopsy showed that my cancer did not go into remission. My blood counts have not returned and I have been given daily blood transfusions. My medical options to treat AML have been exhausted and there is very little that can be done for me now.

Since I really have nothing to lose at this point, I agreed to participate in a clinical study. The drug has not been approved by the FDA to treat leukemia, but it has shown some success in preventing the spread of cancer cells in multiple myeloma patients. It is now being studied in limited leukemia patients who are in my situation. Obviously, there are no statistics or prognosis that can be given to me.

As I keep myself well-guarded, with the few exceptions of occasionally venting when I'm frustrated, I feel most of you don't really know me. I play with my cards close to my chest. However, I had always hoped that I conducted myself in a certain manner that exhibited honesty, hard work, doing the right thing as my conscience and faith dictated, and the ability to not let circumstances derail my goals.

Everyone who is reading this has played some role in any success I may have accomplished on this earth. I have tremendous gratitude and appreciation for those who have helped me and who have opened doors for me that otherwise would have remained shut. This may be my last chance to communicate with you, so I wanted to make sure I took the opportunity while I have the ability to do so.

Some of you may not be aware that I am the only person in my direct lineage to go on to college, and both sets of my grandparents did not make it farther than 6th grade. Three weeks prior to my cancer coming back, I began working as a consultant for the largest political consulting firm in the Midwest. This was my dream career path and something I couldn't have imagined being possible when I graduated high school less than 10 years ago or even undergrad 4 years ago. When tragedy hits and the illusion that we are in control of our lives disappears, it is easy to question God as to why he has let unfair things happen. It's very easy to have faith when things are perfect; it becomes more difficult when things seem hopeless.

Throughout this entire ordeal, I have had moments of despair and uncertainty. They were only moments. My faith in God has endured. I probably have different religious views from many of you as I don't believe in pre-destination but man's own free will to accept or turn away from the Creator. That being said, I do however believe that God does alleviate suffering and that sometimes there is a Divine purpose behind our pain.

When I bow my head in my own personal prayers, I have never asked God to take the cancer away or tried to strike a deal with him to save me. I have only prayed that His will be done.

On his deathbed, a friend asked author and philosopher Henry David Thoreau if he had made peace with God. Thoreau replied, "We have never quarreled."

Live for the glory of God. All other glory is fleeting.

Paul Norman
Consultant-Missouri/Kansas
Victory Enterprises, Inc.
816.812.1613
www.victoryenterprises.com

When I think of Paul and wonder why God took him from us so soon, I reflect on the following quotation and the last line about leaving this world with an imperishable good name. Despite all the pain and suffering Paul had to deal with, he left this world with a good name. Paul also left those who knew him with a good example of how to live.

"In a harbor, two ships sailed: one setting forth on a

*voyage, the other coming home to port. Everyone cheer-ed the ship going out, but the ship sailing in was scarcely noticed. To this a wise man said: 'Do not rejoice over a ship setting out to sea, for you cannot know what ter-rible storms it may encounter and what fearful dangers it may have to endure. Rejoice rather over the ship that has safely reached port and brings its passengers home in peace.'*

*"And this is the way of the world: When a child is born, all rejoice; when someone dies, all weep. We should do the opposite. For no one can tell what trials and travels await a newborn child; but when a mortal dies in peace, we should rejoice, for he has completed a long journey, and there is no greater boon than to leave this world with the imperishable crown of a good name." – The Talmud*

# Chapter 20
# Conclusion

*"Let us hear the conclusion of the whole matter: Fear God, and keep his commandments: for this is the whole duty of man. For God shall bring every work into judgment, with every secret thing, whether it be good, or whether it be evil." – Ecclesiastics 12: 13-14*

In the spring of 2010, Bev Peters' dad, Larry Mayberry, passed away while Larry was in prison. I was living with the Peters and went to the funeral. He had been caught distributing meth, and when he was sixty years old he was sentenced to ten years in a federal prison, but he had cancer and only served about three years before he died. I didn't know much about Larry Mayberry, but I was good friends with Bev, and this was a hard day for her. As I sat in the pew waiting for Bro. Mike Harrison to start the service, I was surprised at how many people were there. I didn't expect a big crowd for a drug dealer's funeral. When the preacher walked up to the front, I couldn't help but feel sympathy for how hard it was going to be to preach this memorial service.

By the time Bro. Harrison started his remarks the Happy Zion Baptist Church in Annapolis, Missouri was full. The preacher's message totally caught me by surprise. It turned out he was a friend of Mr. Mayberry when they were younger. He said that he had tried to talk to Larry about God many times over the years but Larry had always brushed him off.

He started by telling us about Larry's business success and how hard he worked. He said he was always rushing everywhere and never took a break. Larry had come to Iron County with nothing but a mule, but through his hard work and sound investments, he became a very successful businessman. He was in the timber business, and at one time Mr. Mayberry was the second largest employer in Iron County. Many of the people attending the funeral had worked for Larry over the years.

Then the preacher told us that Larry also partied hard. Bro. Harrison said, "We all know about Larry's mistakes." He talked about the drugs and the meth and all the problems Larry got into and how it destroyed his business and ended up sending him to prison. He went on to tell about his prison visits with Larry every Saturday in Jackson, Missouri, before he was sent to a federal prison after his trial. Surprisingly, he revealed that Larry had gotten saved in jail.

After his salvation the preacher said Larry also prayed hard. He told us that Larry had a list of his friends who were not saved that he prayed every day. He explained that Larry was worried that his life had not been a good example to his friends and he wanted them to be saved. Larry would even make him promise to go by and personally talk to certain friends about salvation on behalf of Larry. At that point Bro. Harrison looked out and said, "I have talked to many of you who are here today, and there are others who are here that Larry had on his list."

Then he told us how one Saturday during their visit he told Larry, "I sure hate it that you had to go to jail. It's a shame that you are in here." He said Larry stopped and said, "Oh Mike, don't be sad that I had to go to jail. I'm so thankful for being in jail. Without jail, I never would have been saved and I would have gone on partying and died and gone to hell."

The church got real quiet when he said that. The preacher just looked at us all and didn't say a word for quite some time. I was still in the middle of my troubles, but that story really made me think. I felt like I understood what Mr. Mayberry was talking about. Without my problems, I would have never changed my ways, and changing my ways has brought me a joy I never experienced before my troubles.

I pray you don't have to have the kind of troubles I have had, and I doubt that anyone reading this book has made as many mistakes as me, but we all make mistakes. We are all sinners. Writing a book admitting all my weaknesses and mistakes has not been fun. But on December 7, 2009, just like King David, I made a promise to God when I read Psalms 51. I promised Him I would give Him praise and that I would do my best to help teach transgressors His ways in order to help them avoid my mistakes, if He would rescue me from my troubles. Thankfully, God did exactly what I asked Him to do!

I don't know that I am qualified to teach anyone anything, but I can encourage, pray for and warn others not to make the same mistakes I made. So, figuratively, I've touched the hot stove and burned my hand badly. I don't want any of my friends to experience any of the pain I have experienced, so I will close by pointing out a few lessons I hope my readers picked up from my mistakes.

**1. God loves you.** No matter what you have done, God will forgive you. I have broken all His commandments, and as my testimony shows He still loves me and has blessed me in so many amazing ways. Jesus was praying for the very people who were crucifying Him as He died on the cross. If Jesus did that for them, He will forgive you as well.

**2. Satan is real and has a plan to keep you out of heaven.** Satan is patient and will use your weaknesses and your strengths to get you. For some, Satan brings success so you get busy and don't think you need God. For others, he brings troubles so you get mad at God, and for some he brings guilt so you think God won't love you. I have experienced and succumbed to all of these tricks.

**3. Forgive others and fight being judgmental.** This can happen fast, before we even realize it, but judging others leads to bitterness and unforgiveness.

Bitterness only hurts the person who is bitter. It will cause a lot of problems. Even worse, the Bible says we will be judged in the same way we judge others. I have found that to be very true.

**4. Ignore judgmental Christians who are keeping you from God.** Why would you want to let somebody who is doing something wrong be the reason you miss heaven? This is another scheme of the devil. Satan sometimes uses church people to keep the people who need to be in church out. I promise you, there are more Christians who will welcome you in than there are those who will judge and gossip about you! I learned this firsthand.

**5. Be careful when you compare yourself to others.** I started comparing myself to others and decided that I was not so bad. Everyone makes mistakes and others will almost always fail, but even though I was the biggest hypocrite around I focused more on other's mistakes than my own. There is only one person I should have compared myself to: Jesus Christ. Instead I picked out others who were "worse" than me to help justify my actions.

**6. Watch out for pride.** First, pray and ask the Lord to give you the grace to see your shortcomings and keep you humble. Secondly, ask family and friends who you trust to honestly point out your shortcomings. Then listen to them and don't bite their heads off for being honest with you. Lastly, pay attention to the criticism of your enemies. While you can't let their attacks depress you, I have learned that small kernels of truth can be found in their criticisms and those kernels can sometimes help you see your own faults.

**7. Pray each day.** Ask God to forgive you for your sins and to help you with your needs. When you get too busy to pray, be careful, because pride is probably growing. My problems started when I got too busy and stopped praying.

**8. Give to others.** Don't be greedy. Help others whenever you can, you never know when you will need help too. If you find you don't have time to help others or don't have the compassion or desire to help, be careful; bitterness has probably taken root. I started out as a very helpful and caring person but in the end I became very selfish.

**9. Never have more than two drinks in public.** If you drink in public, stop at two. More than that and your judgment falters. You will say and do things that embarrass you or cause others to lose respect for you. Many of my worst mistakes came after two drinks.

**10. Stay in touch with your friends.** Life can be fun, but it's hard to truly enjoy a happy life without friends. At some point you will need a friend and your friends will need you. When that time comes, and if you've lost touch with your friends, they may not be there when you need them most. Take time to be a good friend. I lost touch with many of my "old" friends who could have kept me grounded.

**11. Avoid the small sins.** Taking the wrong path starts with little sins. They don't seem very bad, but just like the "big" ones, they still separate you from God and always lead to bigger sins. They also seem to be targeted to a person's personal weaknesses. These "small" sins can be things like envy, jealousy, guilt, unforgiveness, fear, pride, bitterness, wrath, lust, worry, etc.... They seem small because they don't appear to hurt anyone else, but if left unchecked they will lead to problems that hurt you and others. These are called besetting sins for a reason. They beset (attack) a person, and ignoring them can lead to a fall. My troubles started with small mistakes that didn't seem that bad.

**12. Obey God's commands.** Read the Bible and learn God's commandments. You cannot obey what you do not know and His commands will help you avoid trouble. Jesus said all the commandments hang on loving God and loving our neighbor as ourselves. If you think about it, how many people get in trouble for loving God and loving their neighbor as they love themselves? Those two commands never got me in trouble, but getting drunk, fornicating, judging others and satisfying my lusts have caused me serious problems.

**13. Remember what is most important.** When life gets too busy to pray, attend church, spend time with family, help others or stay connected to friends, be careful. Even "good" projects and endeavors will take our focus off what is most important and allow us to drift away from faith and family. Being busy doing good things started me down my path to destruction, and I thought I was doing the right thing the whole time.

**14. Turn back to God when He offers.** God gives you opportunities to come to Him, but many times you tell yourself, "I'll do it later," or "I'm not doing anything that bad." Or you ask yourself, "What will I tell my friends?" The longer you run away from God the harder it is to turn back. None of us knows how much time we have, and at some point the opportunities run out. I had many, but I turned them all down. Who knows if I hadn't changed when I did what would have happened. Maybe this book is your opportunity.

**15. Forgive yourself.** Someday you will make a mistake. Hopefully yours will not be as bad or as public as mine, but you will make one. When that day comes think about how important it is to forgive yourself. It's hard to be happy when you hate yourself.

**16. Never give up.** Don't let pain, mistakes or setbacks cause you to give up. No matter what you are trying to do, the one quality that can overcome any obstacle is perseverance. If you are still breathing, God has a plan for you. Keep trying, keep fighting and stay positive. As a Dallas Cowboy receiver, Michael Irvin said, "Get up, look up, and don't ever give up." No matter what your problems are or how bad you think you have messed your life or your family's life up, just remember this old Turkish quotation: "No matter how far you have gone on the wrong road, turn back." Trust me. You can turn everything around and enjoy life again. Just like success and the good times, "This too shall pass."

For me, one of the saddest things about my story is how I let success change me. Flattery, power and prominence caused me to become prideful, paranoid and bitter. Those traits led to all my problems, and while my problems were very embarrassing, knowing that I was not strong enough to handle success and that I let it change me, is the most embarrassing aspect of my story.

Those who do not have faith in God may think my religious talk is only for weak-minded leaders or those who have deep character flaws. But I have found that all of us are susceptible to these temptations. I freely admit my weaknesses. Success and my failures taught me how helpless I am at overcoming temptations. Success caused me to become a very selfish person, but after my troubles my family and friends have told me I'm a much better father, son and friend. Only when God humbled me and Jesus sent his saving grace and mercies was I able to change.

God has given me peace to help me enjoy each day here on earth, but things don't always go as planned and temptations still come. I still have tendencies to be judgmental, hold grudges or lose my patience with others. I have to fight lusts and desires, as well as the temptation to put too much emphasis on popularity and prominence. Of course, I pray each day for the Lord to keep me humble as I fight my old enemy: Pride. Instead of trying to overcome these temptations by myself I now ask the Lord for help, and while I am far from perfect...with God, all things are possible.

Here is a poem I love to think about that helps me stay focused on putting others first and being a better person each day.

### The Work You Did Today
Is anybody happier, because you passed this way?
Does anyone remember, that you spoke to him today?
The day is almost over, and toiling time is through;
Is there anyone to utter, a kindly word for you?
Can you say tonight in parting, with the day that's
     slipping fast?
That you helped a single brother, of the many that you
     passed?
Is a single heart rejoicing, over what you did and said?
Does a man, whose hopes are fading, now with courage
     look ahead?
Did you waste the day or use it, was it well or poorly
     spent?
Did you leave a trail of kindness, or a scar of
     discontent?
As you close your eyes in slumber;
Do you think that God will say?
You have earned one more tomorrow....By the work
     you did today.
– Anonymous

# Chapter 21
# Friends Don't Let Friends Miss Heaven

*"When I say unto the wicked, Thou shalt surely die; and thou givest him not warning, nor speakest to warn the wicked from his wicked way, to save his life; the same wicked man shall die in his iniquity; but his blood will I require at thine hand. Yet if thou warn the wicked, and he turn not from his wickedness, nor from his wicked way, he shall die in his iniquity; but thou hast delivered thy soul. Again, when a righteous man doth turn from his righteousness, and commit iniquity, and I lay a stumbling block before him, he shall die: because thou hast not given him warning, he shall die in his sin, and his righteousness which he hath done shall not be remembered; but his blood will I require at thine hand. Nevertheless if thou warn the righteous man, that the righteous sin not, and he doth not sin, he shall surely live, because he is warned; also thou hast delivered thy soul." – Ezekiel 3:18-21*

Penn Jillette from the magic act "Penn and Teller," is an atheist who wrote the bestseller God, No!: Signs You May Already Be an Atheist and Other Magical

Tales. He is so staunch in his beliefs that he says, "I cross the word 'God' off of every (dollar) bill I touch." There is a YouTube video where Penn talks about how impressed he was by a man who gave him a Bible after one of his shows. The video caught my attention because it was a Gideon Bible the man gave to Jillette, and I am a member of the Gideons. Penn talked about this big guy who was waiting to see him after the show, and he came up and was very complimentary about the show and the language Penn used.

Penn explained the encounter this way: "He said nice stuff. Then he said, 'I brought this for you,' as he handed me a small Gideon pocket edition of the New Testament...He said, 'I wrote in the front of it and wanted you to have this. I'm kind of proselytizing, I'm a businessman, I'm sane, I'm not crazy.' He looked me right in the eye and did all this. It was really wonderful. I believe he knew that I was an atheist, but he was not defensive and he looked me right in the eyes, and he was truly complimentary. It didn't seem like empty flattery. He was really kind and nice and sane and looked me in the eyes, and talked to me and then gave me this Bible. I've always said that I don't respect people who don't proselytize. I don't respect that at all. If you believe that there is a Heaven and a Hell, and people could be going to Hell, or not getting eternal life, or whatever, and you think that, well it's not really worth telling them this because it would make it socially awkward...How much do you have to hate somebody to not proselytize? How much do you have to hate somebody to believe that everlasting life is possible and not tell them that? I mean if I believed beyond a shadow of a doubt that a truck was going to hit you and you didn't believe it and that truck was bearing down on you, there is a certain point where I tackle you, and this is more important than that...This guy was a really good guy. He was polite and honest and sane and he cared enough about me to proselytize and give me a Bible." Here is the link to the video if you would like to watch it yourself:

http://www.youtube.com/watch?v=ZhG-tkQ_Q2w

So, in writing a book to help others learn lessons from my mistakes without making sure you are going to heaven would mean I had left the most important lesson out. My dad always implored others not to let their friends miss heaven. This was dad's motto and his number one goal in life.

If you have read this book and made it to this point, you are my friend and I don't want you to miss heaven. You may already be saved and assured of your place in heaven, but if you have never made the decision to ask Jesus Christ into your life, or you have strayed away from your faith and wonder if you will be in heaven when your life here on earth ends, why not make sure today?

Like me, many people are tricked into thinking they can live "good" lives, try their best, and make it to heaven. Even though they have never made the most important decision of their life, they genuinely believe that they are headed to heaven. Romans 3:23 says, "For all have sinned, and come short of the glory of God." Then, in Romans 6:23 it says, "The wages of sin is death; but the gift of God is eternal life through Jesus Christ our Lord."

Thankfully, God loves us and sent His son to die for us on the cross. As Romans 5:8 says, "But God commendeth his love toward us, in that while we were yet sinners Christ died for us." My testimony proves that no matter what you have done or how many sins you have committed, God still loves you. John 3:16 is a famous verse because it explains God's love and his forgiveness very simply, "For God so loved the world, that he gave his only begotten Son, that whosoever believeth in him should not perish but have everlasting life."

All you have to do is ask. He said in Revelation 3:20 "Behold I stand at the door, and knock: if any man hear my voice, and open the door, I will come in." You can make sure of your salvation right now by praying this simple prayer:

**Dear Jesus, I believe that you died on the cross for my sins and rose on the third day. I confess that I am a sinner and trust you to forgive me and cleanse me from all unrighteousness. I now receive and confess you as my personal Lord and Savior.**

It almost seems too easy, but your faith and that prayer are all it takes to be with God in heaven. Maybe you prayed that prayer long ago when you were a child but, like me, you took a wrong turn and have gotten entangled in a world of sin.

You may feel that God wouldn't take you back after all of the bad things you have done, but He will. Don't just believe me, believe God's word. Look at 1 John 1:9, "If we confess our sins he is faithful and just to forgive us our sins and cleanse us from all unrighteousness." God also says, in 2 Chronicles 7:14, "If my people, which are called by my name, shall humble themselves, and pray, and seek my face, and turn from their wicked ways; then will I hear from heaven, and will forgive their sin, and will heal their land."

I know how hard it is to turn back to God. Leaving friends or addictions behind can be difficult. Wondering what everyone will think about you is scary, but heaven is reserved for overcomers. "He that overcometh shall inherit all things; and I will be his God and he will be my son. But the fearful, and unbelieving, and the abominable, and murderers, and whoremongers, and sorcerers, and idolaters and all liars, shall have their part in the lake which burneth with fire and brimstone: which is the second death" (Revelation 21:7). I beg you to throw your pride away, humble yourself, and ask God to forgive your sins. The joy, happiness and healing you will receive once Jesus sets you free is impossible to describe in words.

# Chapter 22
# Further Study

*"Live as if you were going to die tomorrow. Learn as if you were going to live forever." – Mahatma Gandhi*

I will pass on to you some wise advice dad gave me about reading spiritual books, right after I turned back to the Lord. He said, "Make sure you spend the most time reading and rereading the Bible as you study and search for God's plan in your life." In all my years of attending church, I had never read the Bible through even once before my troubles. Since that time, I have read through the Bible four times. I try to read my Bible each day and find that no matter how many times I read it, I learn something new each time.

There are many good books to read that will bring you closer to the Lord and help you understand His commandments and His plan for your life. I thought I would list a few here that have been extremely helpful to me:

1. The Holy Bible
2. "Abide In Christ" by Andrew Murray
3. "When Christians Suffer" by Thomas Case

4. "Temptation Resisted & Repulsed" by John Owen
5. "The Complete Works of E. M. Bounds on Prayer" by E.M. Bounds
6. "With Jesus Christ in the School of Prayer" by Andrew Murray
7. "Still Standing, 8 Winning Strategies for Facing Tough Times" by James Merritt
8. "The Mischief of Sin" by Thomas Watson
9. "Born Again" by Chuck Colson
10. "The Journey of One Common Man" by Charles Shockley
11. "Humility" by Andrew Murray
12. "The Mortification of Sin" by John Owen

# One Last Request

If reading about God's grace in my life has encouraged you to get closer to the Lord, please send me a note. Your testimony would be a great encouragement to me and I would love to hear what God is doing in your life:

Rod Jetton
rodjetton@gmail.com

# Acknowledgments

*"Faithful are the wounds of a friend, But the kisses of an enemy are deceitful." – Proverbs 27:6*

I would never have had to write a book like this had I listened to my family and friends when they tried to keep me on the right path. My life would have turned out differently, and I would have avoided mistakes, saving myself and them tons of heartache. But I didn't, and while the mistakes and heartache were rough, there are a few benefits to be had from going through troubles.

One of the benefits of my troubles was learning who my true fiends are. Without the Lord and my friends, I never could have survived my mistakes. This acknowledgment section may be a bit longer than normal, but these people helped me when I needed their help most. I don't believe I would be alive to write this book if not for the friends who kept me encouraged after my fall. God sent my friends into my life just when I needed them most, and I owe everything to Him and them!

Jason Crowell is my best friend and has always stood by me, even when I didn't follow his advice. In the movie *Tombstone*, Doc Holliday, the lightning quick, fast-drawing gun slinger, decided to help out his friend, Wyatt Earp, when Wyatt had very few allies. One of the bad guys, Turkey Creek Jack Johnson, asked, "Why you doin' this, Doc?" To which Doc replied, "Because Wyatt Earp is my friend."

"Friend, hell, I got lots of friends."

"Well I don't."

Friends like Jason Crowell are rare. Jason and I fought a lot of fights together. Sometimes I was helping him, and sometimes he was helping me and many of those times we were all by ourselves. In hindsight, we would have been wiser not to have been in some of those fights, but I always knew I could count on him and I knew that, no matter what, he would always be my friend. Proverbs says, "There is a friend who sticks closer than a brother," and Jason Crowell is like a brother to me!

My executive assistant, Kay Fitzpatrick, was such a blessing to me. I know God sent her my way to help get me on the right path, and Lord knows she tried! She and her husband Craig were so very kind to me in the good and bad times. I didn't deserve all their kind-heartedness, but it was much appreciated.

Eric Brookes turned down a $40,000 job to take a $1,000 gig as my driver back in 2004. He wanted to change the world and thought helping me would be the best way to do it. He went from my driver to database manager to operations manager to my partner. Like me, he is the son of a preacher, but unlike me he is an overcomer. I have never seen Eric do anything wrong. He is hardworking, caring and kind. He saw my mistakes but never judged. Eric did exactly what the Bible says in 2 Timothy 2: 24-26, "A servant of the Lord must not quarrel. Instead, he must be kind to everyone. He must be a good teacher. He must be willing to suffer wrong. He must be gentle in correcting those who oppose the Good News. Maybe God will allow them to change the way they think and act and lead them to know the truth. Then they might come back to their senses and God will free them from the devil's snare so that they can do his will." GOD'S WORD. Eric was patient and kind and gently prodded me in the right direction while he prayed for God to give me grace to come to my senses.

I also want to thank my staff members who saw my life spiraling out of control and bravely tried to nudge me in the right direction: Allene Howser, Shane Schoeller, Chris Benjamin, Keith Kirk, Aaron Willard, Don Lograsso, Betty Pringer, Wayne Yokam, and, in particular, Dave Hageman. They are such wonderful people and were responsible for much of my professional success. They tried to help, but I didn't listen and I know I let them down.

John Bardgett had no reason to stop my self-destruction and, as a lobbyist, his self-interest was not in advising me on personal matters, but he was daring enough to warn me of the problems I was getting into. Then, after my fall, he graciously helped me when friends were hard to find. I will forever be indebted to him and his wife, Kim, for their kindness. Jorgen Schlemeier, Bill and Cindy Gamble, Guy Black, Sam Licklider, Shannon Cooper, Kent Gains, Jon Dolan, Nancy Giddens, Travis Brown, Kathi Harness, Lynn Schlosser, and Brent Hemphill were also very kind to me after my fall.

Christine Gordon was a phenomenal fundraiser and we developed a close friendship over the years. When on the road, I basically lived at her house in St. Louis and her husband, Steve, welcomed me into their family. They both had long talks with me about life while watching Cardinal games. I should have taken more of their advice.

Nicole Brown, Shawn Bell, Cherie Snyder, Dan Klinesorge and Eric Brooks all lost their jobs when I had to suddenly shut down my campaign consulting company, but each of them offered comfort and kindness even though my mistakes had caused them so much trouble.

Reps. Rex Rector and Ed Emery took time to do a Bible study with me each week, and I now wish I would have opened up to them and explained my struggles more. Kerry Messer was also a good example in the Capitol and someone I should have confided in. I had many other friends who would have helped me had I asked, but I did everything I could to keep my troubles hidden and away from prying eyes. In politics I felt I couldn't afford to look weak and if my enemies would have heard about a potential problem they would have done everything they could to exploit it.

Steven Tilley, who was Speaker of the Missouri House at the time of my fall, never abandoned our friendship, even when I told him to run far away. I didn't want my mistakes to hurt my friends, but Steven never seemed to care. Charles Skoda is another person who offered advice, encouragement, and help when I needed it most. He is an old Navy fighter pilot, and I was very thankful to have the Navy taking care of me again!

David and Bev Peters live out in the woods of Bollinger County and were kind enough to let me move into their basement. They have a beautiful log home that I nicknamed the "lodge" and spending time with their family in early 2010 was such a blessing.

I cannot describe how helpful Scott Muschany's council was as I dealt with my shattered life. His wife, Harriet, allowed me to spend lots of time with their family in St. Louis and I am convinced that Harriet is an angel living here on earth. Scott also introduced me to pastor Ed Kleiman who offered some wonderful spiritual council that helped me get my life back on track. My time with Scott, Harriet and Ed helped point me toward God and repentance.

I also had some "old" friends who I lost touch with who were kind enough to reach out and encourage me. Tom Burcham, Bob Behnen, Chris Blaylock, Charles Brazeale, Odel Stearling, Scott Faughn, Melissa Grissom, Russ Oliver, John Robinson, Lea Behlmann, Clyde Lear, Keri Ryerson, Steve and Patty Boyers, Jewell Filer, Reva Collins, Peter Kinder, Mavis Busiek,

Steve Plaster, Greg and Angie West, Sam Richardson, Dana Rademan, Delton Dees, Marilyn Miller, Peter Herschend, Lloyd Smith, Lisa Reitzel, Ron Casey, Tim Drury, Larry Weis, Menlo Smith, Gary Black, Joan Branson, Marilyn Seaton, Logan Thompson, Kathy White, Jeff Small, Jeff Roe, Rob and Nancy Mayer, Reid Forrester, Ryan McKenna, Bill McKenna, Doug Albrecht, Cheryl Counts, Elijah Allen, Keith Buck, Jim Dyke, Connie and Skip Sayersbrook, Jim and Wanda Dusek, David Day, Kellie Tilley, Ray Rowland, Billy Pat Wright, Bob and Patty Ingold, John Hancock, Stan Schultz, Bill Foster, Steve Vester, Adam Crumbliss, Monte Collins, Lis Smith, Steve Bradford, David Barklage, John Pierce, Joe, Cathy and Katy Forand, Robin and Scott Lady, Gary Rust, Lister Florence, and Marsha Pope are just a few of the friends who encouraged me. There were many others who probably don't want to be recognized (some are still in office), but I still cherish each card, text, email or call of encouragement I received.

There are also those who quietly prayed for me when I needed prayer the most. I have learned about many of you since my troubles, but for those I don't know about, THANK YOU...the Lord answered those prayers. I will forever be in debt to all those who took time to pray for a lost and confused sinner like me.

My new friends at Schultz and Summers Engineering were very kind to me despite my checkered past. Coworkers like Brad Allbritton, Bob Summers, Amanda LaPorte, Jaymie Mitchell, Debbie Norris, Ron Jungbauer, Jim Burtin, Wayne Faries, Jim Fisher, Marvin Nesbit, Kendal Barks, Lance Cravens, Ashley Mattli, Sammi Croy, Jeremy Conover and Bari Chase all accepted me when I joined their team.

While my friends helped me survive the hard times, this book would not have been possible without the help of my editor, Rob Bignell. His experience and knowledge of the publishing process has made this task so much easier. Scott Lady, along with Peter and Sue Westrum, were also kind enough to read the manuscript and offer very helpful suggestions. In addition, I want to thank Nanda Olney for her ability to help me find the right words to convey some very difficult experiences. When I was stuck on a thought or my sentences sounded rough, she helped me find just the right word and smoothed all the rough edges off. Furthermore, Michelle K. Tandy proved invaluable at finding unseen errors that needed fixing. Her editing skills arrived just in the nick of time. Of course, without Jonathan Miller and the Recovering Politician's willingness to publish my writings, this book would never have been printed.

# Photo Collage

Speaker Pro-Tem Carl Bearden, Floor Leader Tom Dempsey and Rodney Jetton on the dais.

My daughters Callie and Emily serving as House pages for the day.

Budget talks during a joint leadership meeting with (L to R) Rep. Jason Crowell, Rep. Rod Jetton, Rep. Carl Bearden, Speaker Catherine Hanaway, Sen. Mike Gibbons, Sen. John Russell and President Pro-Tem Peter Kinder.

John Bardgett and I attending a Cardinals game after my troubles were behind me.

Catherine Hanaway's Chief of Staff, Chuck Casiley, teaching at a campaign school in 2002.

Governor Holden and Rodney Jetton discussing transportation issues in 2002.

Rodney Jetton with Ann Wagner and John Hancock
receiving the Legislator of the Year award from Missouri
Pachyderms.

Kay Fitzpatrick and Rodney Jetton on the dais.

Mark Richardson (standing) showing Rodney Jetton the ropes in 2001.

Rodney Jetton's mother and father, Frank & Marie James, Clinton & Tammy Gross, and Debbie Bearden at the 2007 swearing in ceremony.

(L to R) David Sater, Mark Wright, Dennis Woods, Bob Dixon, Mike Cunningham, Rod Jetton, Maynard Wallace, Brad Roark, BJ Marsh, Larry Wilson, Jack Goodman, Mike Parson and Don Wells at the MU name change bill signing.

The Speaker's key staff in 2005 (L to R) Chris Dunn, Fay Fitzpatrick, Arron Willard, Tina Bernskoetter, Rod Jetton, Betty Pringer, Chris Benjamin, Zach Monroe.

The new 90-member Republican majority on November 6, 2002.

Dave Schwab, Billy Pat Wright, JoAnn Emerson, Rob Mayer, Rodney Jetton at a fundraiser for Billy Pat.

Reps. Ted Hoskins, Carl Bearden, Rod Jetton, Steve Hunter, Rodney Hubbard, Curt Dougherty, TD El-Amin, Scott Muschany, and Ed Robb at a school choice press event.

(L to R) Jason Van Eaton, John Hancock, Chuck Caisley, Ann Wagner, Speaker Catherine Hanaway, Eric Feltner, Scott Baker, Rich Chrismer, Senator David Klint, and Rod Jetton at the Republican Party planning session in 2002.

Governor Blunt and Speaker Rod Jetton meet with Missouri
National Guardsmen securing the boarder close to Yuma,
Arizona.

The Nieves, Beardens, Shannon Cooper, Cassie and Rodney
Jetton, Brad Roark, Goodmans, Ruestmans, and Rectors
posing for a photo.

(L to R) Peter Meyers, Lanie Black, Rob Mayer, Mark
Richardson, Denny Meredith and Bill Foster meeting about
issues effecting Southeast Missouri. This group was
unofficially dubbed the "Boothill Mafia."

(L to R) Shannon Cooper, Dr. Wayne Cooper, Bob Dixon, Rod
Jetton, John Quinn, Farm Bureau President Charlie Kruse,
Therese Sanders, Bob Behnen, Kathy Chinn, Jim Guest, and
Lanie Black at the Farm Bureau lobby day.

Rodney Jetton and Jason Crowell after a goose hunt.

(L to R) Nathan Dampf, Kay Fitzpatrick, Kenny Ross, Rodney Jetton, intern Ryan Lewis, Chris Dunn, Betty Pringer, Arron Willard, Don Lagrosso, and Chris Benjamin posing for a staff photo in front of the capitol.

The Republican leadership team (L to R) Caucus Secretary Marilyn Ruestman, Caucus Chairman Bob Dixon, Speaker Rodney Jetton, Speaker Pro-Tem Carl Bearden, Floor Leader Tom Dempsey, and Assistant Floor Leader Tom Self.

Rodney Jetton with two of his key staff members, (L to R) Keith Kirk and Dave Hageman.

(L to R) Rodney Jetton, Cathy Chinn, Will Kraus, Rachel Storch, Mike Dethrow, Gayle Kingery, John Quinn, Melba Curls and Therese Sander at a bi-partisan press conference.

Rodney Jetton with Judiciary Chairman Richard Byrd who sadly passed away in 2005.

Most of the members of the 2000 class who led the drive to win the majority. Back row (L to R), Bob Behnen, Shannon Cooper, Steve Hunter. Center row, Carl Bearden, Tom Dempsey, Rex Rector Richard Byrd. Bottom row, Rodney Jetton, Jane Cunningham, Danie Moore, Jason Crowell, Kathlyn Fares, and John Quinn.

Marines in the Missouri House (L to R) Barney Fisher, Jim Avery, Rodney Jetton, Gary Dusenburg, Jack Jackson and Navy Corpsman Brian Nieves.

Jason Crowell and Rodney Jetton talking strategy on the dais.

Rodney Jetton and Rules Chairman Shannon Cooper talking on the House floor.

(L to R) Kevin Wilson, Carl Bearden, Sen. Dan Clemens, Bill Deeken, Mark Bruns, Governor Blunt, Economic Development Director Greg Stinhoff, Rod Jetton and Senate President Pro-Tem Mike Gibbons.

Rodney Jetton and Speaker Catherine Hanaway on the dais.

Speaker Pro-Tem Rodney Jetton talks floor strategy with
Majority Leader Jason Crowell in 2003.

Speaker Rodney Jetton being sworn in by Supreme Court
Chief Justice Stephen Limbaugh, while Cassie Jetton holds
the Bible in 2005.

Rodney Jetton with his son Will Jetton on the dais in 2005.

Bill Jetton opens the House in prayer while Secretary of
State Matt Blunt looks on in 2005.

Speaker Rodney Jetton holding an unprecedented joint press conference to highlight the key issues in 2005 with Minority Leader Jeff Harris, Assistant Minority Leader Paul LeVota, Minority Whip Connie Johnson, Minority Caucus Secretary Terry Young and Wes Wagner.

Speaker Rodney Jetton being escorted into the House chamber to be sworn in by Martin Rucker, Bob Behnen, Kenny Jones, Richard Byrd, and Judy Baker.

Rodney Jetton talking with the press after his walk to Jefferson City in 2001.  Reps. Wes Shoemyer, Brad Roark and Steve Henderson also attended.

# COMING IN 2015

# "7 PITFALLS OF POWER"

## by Rodney Jetton

### PREFACE

Many interesting things have been said about power, and most of them aren't very positive. That's probably because most men and women throughout history haven't been wise in their handling of power. In far too many instances, power ends up controlling the person who possesses it instead of the person in power being able to control it.

One of the most well-known quotations about power comes from Lord Acton, who said, "Power corrupts and absolute power corrupts absolutely." Many famed historians have given credence to that thought. The pages of human history are littered with stories about rulers, presidents, preachers, CEOs and other leaders who let power corrupt their souls, causing pain and destruction to the very people they were responsible for leading.

Others have said it's not power that corrupts but the fear of losing power that causes many leaders to put self-interest in front of serving those for whom they're responsible. President Lincoln observed, "Nearly all men can stand adversity, but if you want to test a man's character, give him power." Missouri Sen. Jason Crowell continued with that line of thought when he said, "Power doesn't always corrupt, but it does always reveal."

The *7 Pitfalls of Power* were written to point out a few of the potential risks authority can lead to. While most books about power are focused on how to obtain it or use it, the *7 Pitfalls of Power* is different. Hopefully, this book will illustrate some of the potential pitfalls power can cause not only to those who possess it, but also to those who are striving to attain it. While I don't want to dismiss the pain those in authority can cause the people they lead, the primary focus of this book is to discuss the hazards of power and to emphasize the personal peril power can present to those in charge. I hope to warn well-intentioned leaders about how power can change the person who holds it, because power is a volatile commodity, much like dynamite. Those who wield power must handle it with wisdom, humility and care. If handled wisely, power will benefit both the person who has it and those they are leading or influencing. But when handled unwisely, power can destroy a leader and greatly harm those he or she leads.

In the Marine Corps, we would sometimes use

dynamite to blow through a minefield, take down a bridge, or clear debris off a roadway. Dynamite is small but very powerful, and when used properly it was a wonderful tool for assisting us in carrying out our mission. But we had to go through training to use dynamite correctly. We had to learn the proper way to use it and the dangers of improperly using it.

Too much in the wrong place wouldn't do what we intended, and could backfire, making our job harder. Even worse, if we didn't handle it with care and deploy our charges properly, the explosion could kill us.

Like dynamite, power has the potential to harm those who are using it the most. Proper training is required to wield power wisely. Ideally, a new leader seeks a powerful position in order to accomplish a worthwhile goal. Unfortunately, in many instances, they have neither the experience nor the wisdom to avoid the harmful side effects of power.

In the pages that follow, I'll use many of my personal experiences, as well as those of other influential leaders, to help identify the pitfalls that anyone in a position of powerful leadership should watch out for. We will explore the pitfalls of pride, bitterness, fear, flattery, lack of focus, judgmental attitude, and lust. I chose these seven because as a powerful Speaker of the Missouri House these seven pitfalls caused me to stumble and fall.

Experience can be a tough teacher and the lessons we learn are costly. Hopefully, you will gain some useful insights by learning from our mistakes. I encourage you to keep this wise old Russian saying in mind as you turn the pages that follow: The wise man learns from someone else's mistakes, the smart man learns from his own, and the stupid one never learns.

## WHAT IS POWER?

*Power n 1: "The ability to act or produce an effect 2: a position of ascendency over others 3: AUTHORITY one who has control or authority; esp: a sovereign state 4: physical might; also mental or moral vigor"* – Merriam-Webster

Before we discuss the pitfalls of power, we should explore the meaning of power and agree to exactly what it is. When we think of power, most of us conjure visions of elected officials, military commanders, corporate CEOs, or law enforcement officers. In short, we normally think of those in authority. These are all powerful positions that we'll discuss in the following chapters, but I want you to consider a more simple definition that's focused on human interactions.

To me, the basic description of power is the ability to get others to do what you want. We also call this influence. The capacity to make others do your bidding is the ultimate manifestation of possessing power. It's is easy to see that military commanders, government leaders, CEOs, policemen, and even parents have control over those under their authority, but physical and mental gifts can also allow individuals to control or influence others.

A few of the characteristics that tend to provide individuals with influence even when they're not in a traditional leadership position, include money, fame, physical abilities, intelligence, orator skills, charm, beauty, subject expertise, trustworthiness, and charisma. While there are many other "talents" we could add to this list, it's clear that these kinds of traits typically allow those who possess them to gain control over their peers through promotions, advancements or even natural selection.

Most leaders are chosen for a position because their particular talent is needed to accomplish a given task. Sometimes those in power promote talented individuals to a position of authority, but other times they're pushed by their peers to take the lead. In both cases, the result is one person gaining the power to control the actions of another person or group of people.

Ancient history is full of examples where strong men rose to power because of their strength, or where smart men used their intellect to overcome adversaries, or even when a woman was able to use her beauty to change the course of human history. While strength alone may not be the determining factor for obtaining power in our modern times, news reports are full of accounts where those with money, fame, charm, knowledge, trust or charisma have used their gifts to gain power over others.

Typically, it takes three ingredients for a person to

obtain power. First, a problem or difficult task exists, then a person with the necessary talents to solve the problem or complete the task is identified. Lastly, that person must have enough ambition or confidence to believe that he or she can lead the effort to accomplish the mission.

The above description sounds so straightforward, idealistic and principled, so you may be wondering why power often has such a bad rap. Throughout history, there are many examples where those who amassed power benefited others and led to progress for human civilizations. If history shows us that someone amassing power and human advancement are connected, then what has caused power to be looked upon with such disdain? Why does it seem that power and progress are so often peppered with corruption, hardship and pain to both leaders and followers? That's the million dollar question. Both history and my personal experience have taught me that gaining power is much easier than keeping it, and that maybe the most difficult task of all is consistently using it wisely.

There's an old saying in politics, "You will never be as popular as you were after you won your first election." The fights, betrayal, and backstabbing, as well as the flattery, butt-kissing and gift giving along with countless personal attacks can cause well-intentioned leaders to lose focus on the main goal or even why they sought power over others in the first place. Of course, honest mistakes or a lack of ability can lead to poor decisions and cause problems for both leaders and followers, but all too often self-interest, self-preservation or even basic survival instincts cause leaders to inflict pain on those they lead.

So is power helpful or harmful? Has it done more good than bad? Hard questions to answer, but good questions to ponder. Perhaps the answer depends on the character of the person who possess power, which will require each of us to take a hard and honest look deep into our souls. If you are in a position of power or diligently working to gain a position of power, what will power reveal about your character?     Perfect power...it's an oxymoron at best.

## ABOUT THE AUTHOR

Rodney Jetton is a former Speaker of the Missouri House and a
skilled communicator who has
candidly shared his personal
story of success, failure and forgiveness with elected officials,
Christian men's groups, student
assemblies and church audiences all across America. He
currently owns Targeted Com-

munications, a content market-ing company helping
businesses build better relation-ships with their
customers. He also is a partner in Sec-ond Act
Strategies, a bipartisan group of former public servants
who share their stories of overcoming crises with
corporations, elected officials, and not-for-profit
organizations. Rodney served as the marketing director for Schultz Surveying and Engineering Inc. from
2010 to 2013 where he helped double the company's
revenues allowing SSE to make the Inc. 500/5000 list
in 2010, 2011 and 2012. Rodney was recognized by the
*Springfield Business Journal* as the top Marketing Director in Southwest Missouri in 2011. He founded *The
Missouri Times*, Missouri's top newspaper covering
public policy and politics. He most recently finished the
memoir Son of a Preacher Man about his life growing
up in the home of a Baptist preacher. He also co-
authored a book on crisis management, The Recover-

ing Politician's Twelve Step Program to Survive Crisis. Rodney served as a Captain in the United States Marine Corps, and enjoys outdoor activities such as running, hiking, mountain biking, and fishing. He is a member of Gideons International and attends the Sanctuary of Hope Church in Branson, Missouri. Rod is also the father of three wonderful children Callie, Emily and Will. To learn more about him, go to www.rodjetton.com.

*Contact Information*
Rodney Jetton
rodjetton@gmail.com
Linkedin: http://www.linkedin.com/in/rodjetton/
Facebook: https://www.facebook.com/rodjetton
Twitter: https://twitter.com/jedijetton
Website: www.rodjetton.com

## Son of a Preacher Man: Growing up in the Seventies and Eighties

Rodney Jetton grew up in the Seventies and Eighties as the son of a Southern Baptist preacher. Growing up as a pastor's son can be challenging and his autobiography does a great job of providing us with a candid and sometimes humorous look at what goes on after the Sunday sermon.

In this heartwarming narrative, you will get to know the extended Jetton family and share in their triumphs and setbacks. While this book was written for his children, and is full of touching stories, educational illustrations and commonsense advice, it will provide the reader with a unique glimpse into the consequences of the good and bad choices we make daily in our lives.

The first few chapters introduce a lively cast of family members and are filled with childhood memories of Rodney's years growing up. He then takes us through his high school and college years, sharing intimate details about his failure to follow his parent's teachings and God's commandments. Through it all he demonstrates God's capacity to forgive a prodigal son.

Rodney's testimony of God's amazing grace during

the first twenty years of his life will provide comfort and guidance to today's parents trying to raise children and teenagers in a Christian home. Teenagers and young adults will benefit from these frank and easy to read stories on the temptations and challenges they must overcome in today's fast paced world.

## The Recovering Politician's Twelve Step Program to Survive Crisis
*Featured on MSNBC's "Hardball with Chris Matthews" and HuffPost Live!*

Columbia University Prof. Marc Lamont Hill declared: "Make sure you check out this book. It's an awesome book, and a great contribution to the national conversation."

In The Recovering Politician's Twelve Step Program to Survive Crisis, more than a dozen "recovering politicians" share their twelve step program on how to survive crises – from highly publicized and politicized scandals, to smaller, more intimate interpersonal struggles. They outline deliberate, focused and vigorous courses of action and reaction, gleaned from their own experiences – often dramatic, sometimes painful under the piercing lights of the political arena. Crisis management, of course, has captured the zeitgeist: Scandal's Olivia Pope and The Good Wife's Eli Gold have brought the crisis manager to the mainstream; PR firms are racing to rebrand themselves as crisis advisers; and it seems like every Clinton and Bush era senior official is offering his or her wares or writing a book on the subject. Moreover, many of the most widely-read news stories of the past few decades have involved politicians, athletes, and celebrities struggling through crises that involve sex, lies, audiotape, drugs, criminal activity, and/or unethical behavior. Just recently, consider the cases of Lance Armstrong, Manti Te'o, Anthony Weiner, Mark Sanford, David Petraeus, Jesse Jackson, Jr., Penn State football, even Beyonce's lip synching at the presidential inauguration. Most Americans probably view scandal through the prism of ideology, partisanship, or even conspiracy. At the heart, however, are flawed human beings making mistakes, acting emotionally, and desperately trying to preserve their reputations and careers. In The Recovering Politician's Twelve Step Program to Survive Crisis, a diverse, bi-partisan collection of former politicians, draw lessons from their own scandals – ranging from allegations of ethical and sexual impropriety, to suffering through alcoholism and depression, to being censured and forced out of office, to serving time in federal prison – and share their guidance on how everyday readers can transcend crisis, recover, and launch their own second acts.

Made in the USA
Lexington, KY
02 October 2014